he

HOLD

MW00719358

HARMLESS

AGREEMENT

A Management Guide
to Evaluation and Control

4th edition

Georgia Chapter –

Chartered Property and

Casualty Underwriters

NATIONAL
UNDERWRITER

The National Underwriter Co. • 420 East 4th St. • Cincinnati, OH 45202

International Standard Book Number: 0-87218-336-X

Library of Congress Catalog Card Number: 87-60917

The National Underwriter Company
420 East 4th St., Cincinnati 45202

Fourth Edition 1987

Third Printing 1989

Printed in the United States of America

FOREWORD

Since the original publication of this book in 1968 and subsequent revisions in 1973 and 1977, the subject matter covered in this fourth edition has undergone a maturing process. From the original effort to define and explore the subject, to the subsequent effort to identify and evaluate the then current environment, the study has grown to an analysis of areas of special sensitivity which have become apparent.

The principal area of sensitivity (which continues to be most significant) is the legislation which has been enacted to restrict the use of hold harmless agreements. Not only have additional states enacted legislation, but also the nature of such legislation is much more sophisticated in application.

In addition, these statutes have been tested in litigation in many jurisdictions. This process now provides a broader legal basis for consideration which adds new perspective to the study. More importantly, the statutes may well serve as a deterrent to the use of hold harmless agreements as a convenient tool to postpose an understanding until the perceived misunderstanding occurs.

Another sensitive area is the legal distinction between an employe and subcontractor. This legally agonizing problem is often compounded in contractual relationships when this definition becomes the basis of the dispute.

An additional area of sensitivity is in some of the techniques being attempted to handle the risk arising out of assumption of liability under contract. An observation of some of these techniques indicates that there still needs to be a more complete understanding of the proper function of insurance.

The intent of the original study was to make the uninformed aware, the indifferent concerned and those in dispute, mutually understanding. This latest edition is dedicated to the fulfillment of this original intent.

GEORGIA CHAPTER CPCU
Atlanta, Georgia 1987

v

*The Committee is especially grateful for
the untiring efforts of*

W. DAN McDONALD, CPCU

*who undertook the task of revising
the original study. The second and third
editions were the result of his work. His input
to this fourth edition was greatly appreciated.*

ACKNOWLEDGEMENTS

The Georgia Chapter of The Society of Chartered Property and Casualty Underwriters conceived this study in July, 1967, at which time a committee of eight was organized. To our early meetings we invited individuals representing organizations who were vitally concerned with this problem and whom we felt would be of invaluable assistance in our efforts to gather research material. We are indebted to the following individuals:

Robert H. Strickland, Executive Secretary, Georgia Branch, The Associated General Contractors of America, Inc., Atlanta, Georgia

Bernard B. Rothschild, F.A.I.A., Director, South Atlantic Region, American Institute of Architects, Atlanta, Georgia

Overton A. Currie, Smith, Currie and Hancock, Attorneys at Law, Atlanta, Georgia, Chairman, Public Contract Section, Southeastern Region, American Bar Association.

In addition, a special acknowledgement must be made to Ted Carleton, CPCU, a driving force behind many of the research projects of the Georgia Chapter. His untiring efforts in the pursuit of research excellence have been greatly appreciated.

Finally, we wish to express appreciation to the Atlanta Chapter of Risk and Insurance Management Society for its generous contribution. It was through that group's wholehearted cooperation that we were able to obtain a variety of specimen hold harmless agreements which were so vital to this study.

CONTENTS

CHAPTER I

WHY HOLD HARMLESS AGREEMENTS?

Introduction

The three decades following the end of World War II have seen unprecedented sociological and technological readjustments in the world economy. Never before in recorded history have the social, economic and political systems of world society been subjected to such demanding challenges and opportunities.

These challenges and opportunities have truly tested the ability of the private and governmental sectors of this nation to properly allocate classical factors of production—land, labor and capital. The foreseeable future seems to pose an even greater challenge to the private sector of our economy to continue its acceptance and fulfillment of the needs of society.

The rapidity of change which continues to accelerate under these pressures has resulted in a never ending series of negotiations between all the parties to the economic developments within the society. These negotiations have given rise to a dramatic promiscuity of contractual relationships.

Only one phase of these contractual relationships—the hold harmless clause—is treated in this study. Unfortunately, this contractual clause has often heretofore been ignorantly or indifferently overlooked or has been a point of major contention between the contracting parties.

Its consequence may range from an innocuous restatement of common law principles to contractual obligations so serious in nature that their legality may hinge on their being "contrary to public policy."

Definition of Study

This study is intended to place this contractual assumption of another's liability in its proper perspective. By so doing, the uninformed may be made aware; the indifferent may be made concerned and those in dispute may be more understanding.

It is apparent that the use of hold harmless clauses serves more pragmatic purposes than a simple exhibition of strength of bargaining power by one party to the contract. The many considerations involving the decisions to invoke such contractual impositions are enumerated in this chapter.

The design of the hold harmless agreement itself is largely the work of attorneys. The legal aspects of exculpatory clauses are treated in Chapter II. That chapter also provides a commentary on the attention this subject is receiving from the various legislative bodies across the nation.

Once one has seen why hold harmless agreements are being so widely used and the legal environment in which they operate, it is important to see the agreement in actual contract form. Chapter III provides an assortment of the most commonly used indemnity agreements and represents a cross section of various types of agreements from a diverse group of industries. It also provides an analysis of the agreements illustrated.

The control of risk assumption which is created contractually is dealt with in Chapter IV. Criteria are established for contracting parties in their efforts to assure that they have reacted properly to the consequences of the obligation confronting them.

Since insurance is one of the most common methods of funding the liability under contract, space is devoted to the insurance forms available for this purpose. Chapter V covers the contractual liability provisions of the 1/73 edition of the ISO's Comprehensive General Liability Program. Chapter VI is devoted to the treatment of contractual liability in ISO's new Commercial General Liability policy forms. Since some insurers will continue to use the 1/73 edition, both chapters are necessary as a reference. These chapters also contain advice on understanding the terms and conditions of the forms as well as their limitations.

The primary purpose of this study is to bring together in one publication the available comment on this most unique subject. The variety of sources of information for this study and the response received from the many individuals contacted would indicate that this study is actually only a point of departure. The study of hold harmless agreements is a continuing one. If this publication only serves to encourage continued study by those interested, it will have made a significant contribution.

Background

The contractual liability created by the hold harmless agreement is *the assumption, by contract, of another's liability*. It is obvious that such an obligation is either transferred or assumed by a party during contract negotiations. Although not necessarily true, it is often the case that the assumption of another's liability is a demonstration of a weakness in bargaining position.

In all too many situations, this additional obligation is treated as an afterthought by those in negotiation or it may well be inconspicuously located in the formal contract document and never seriously considered.

Since hold harmless agreements are found in almost every phase of contractual relationships, it is important that a description of some of the typical parties to the contract be discussed. This discussion provides the background for the consideration of why these agreements are so often encountered in contract negotiations.

The *indemnitor* is the party to the contract who assumes the obligation to hold the *indemnitee* harmless for liability arising out of the contract. These parties find themselves in a variety of situations when confronted with the decision of the proper application of a hold harmless provision and the reasons for its application.

The indemnitor may be in one of the following contracting situations when the indemnity clause becomes relative in the contract negotiations:

1. The seller of a good or service.

2. The contractor who is performing the production, construction or maintenance of a product or assuming the obligation to perform a service.

3. A subcontractor who is performing the production, construction or maintenance of a product or assuming the obligation to perform a service for a prime contractor.

4. A tenant who is leasing property, equipment or service from another party.

The indemnitee usually finds himself in the contrary position created by these situations:

1. The purchaser of a good or service.

2. An owner for whom a contractor or subcontractor is performing the production, construction or maintenance of a product or assuming the obligation to perform a service.

3. A property owner who is leasing property, equipment or service to another party.

It is in these situations that the indemnitee may be in a bargaining position which provides him with the opportunity to have the liability arising out of the contract assumed by another.

The situations which arise in the application of hold harmless are so complex that those described above are only indicated to serve as a guide. It is not uncommon to find a situation in which the property owner in fact becomes the indemnitor and the lessee becomes the indemnitee. The final determination of which of the parties is to be the indemnitor is usually made at the time the contract is being negotiated. It is under bargaining circumstances that the relative strength of bargaining power is exhibited and the party holding this power can demand indemnity from the other party to the contract.

REASONS FOR USE OF INDEMNITY AGREEMENTS

Bargaining Position of Parties

It should be apparent that the transfer or assumption of liability is subject to the relative position of those who are attempting to achieve preferred treatment for the interest they represent. In most situations, the indemnity agreement will result in an additional cost to the indemnitor whether this be in the form of insuring the assumed liability or the handling of the risk by other means.

Obviously, the addition of any cost will affect the profitability of the transaction unless proper prior arrangements can be made to offset these costs. On the other hand, the indemnitee enjoys the cost advantage of having the costs for handling the risk arising out of the contract passed on to the indemnitor. Ultimately, the indemnitor must evaluate the "after the contract" situation in order that he may give proper respect to his obligations under the contract.

DEFINITION OF LEGAL RESPONSIBILITY

Although the annals of jurisprudence are filled with the doctrine of the laws of negligence, courtrooms are also filled with unpredictable jury verdicts. No party to a contract would prefer the interpretation of the contract by a jury when the very intent of the contract document is to represent a "meeting of the minds" of the parties to it.

By reducing the liability arising out of the contract to a condition of the contract itself, a formal effort is made to properly affix the responsibilities of the parties for claims which may develop in the future. The hold harmless agreement within a contract specifically indicates the effort made by the parties to the contract to make their *mutual understanding* regarding this element a part of the consideration for the contract.

Bringing a suit under contract has distinct advantages for legal adversaries. Such legal implications include:

1. Extension of statute of limitations.

2. Evasion of statutes which may be specific in regard to the legal situations which may result from the contract.

   a. (Illustration) The Illinois Scaffold Act which makes the owner liable when he is in charge of the erection of a building and willfully violates the act.

   b. Political immunities which bar typical tort actions, but not claims under contract.

3. Preclusion of the application of contributory negligence as an element in the adjudication of the claim.

4. Traversing the common law through the assumption of the sole negligence of another.

5. Abrogating the degree of responsibility criteria by creation of more severe legal situation such as substitution of absolute liability for reasonable care.

6. Taking advantage of the distinction between the legal interpretation of indemnity for liability and indemnity against loss.

It becomes apparent that the construction of a hold harmless agreement must be the responsibility of the legal advisers. Chapter II is devoted to the legal implications of this subject and the current statutes applying to these agreements.

EFFECTS OF RISK MANAGEMENT PROGRAMS

Risk managers are charged with the responsibilities of assuring their principals that the business risks within their area of concern are properly treated. The risk arising from contract is surely one of these. The risk manager recognizes that contracts are essential to the usual conduct of business, but the liability arising from these contracts must be evaluated.

In the evaluation of the use of a hold harmless agreement, the risk manager must consider its effect on the methods he is employing to handle the risk of his firm. He should consider the effects on the following problem areas before recommending a course of action for the treatment of a given indemnity agreement:

1. The use of deductibles, risk retention or self-insurance techniques.

2. The effect on insurance cost of a possible claim arising out of the contract.

3. The cost arising out of the failure of the indemnitor to satisfy a judgment for which he has become liable.

4. The effect of the indemnity agreement on the economic desirability of the subject of the contract.

CONCLUSION

Apart from formal risk assumption through a self-insurance plan, the assumption of any risk is usually the result of ignorance or indifference. In the case of the risk of liability assumed under contract, the latter two appear to be the greatest source of the problems created by such liability.

Since the parties to contract vary beyond the scope of imagination, it is not difficult to establish that many of them do not have the personal knowledge or the resources to employ advisers to make them aware of the consequences of this problem. Fortunately for them, they seem to fall in a general class of operators who are recognized for these inadequacies and the other party to the contract provides for this eventuality by providing itself with protection for this contingency.

One method of achieving protection for those who may ignorantly assume liability beyond their resources is the introduction of a surety as a condition of the contract. Under these circumstances, the obligations to the indemnitee-obligee run jointly from the indemnitor-surety. This does not appear to be the most satisfactory solution to the protection of the ignorant, because of the obvious difficulties he may encounter in acquiring a surety bond.

The only sure method for the ignorant to employ is that of seeking advice from either his insurance agent or his attorney or both.

Indifference to the contractual obligation assumed under hold harmless agreements seems to stem from an over-anxiousness to acquire the opportunity afforded by the contract. Too often the realization of the consequence of the obligation comes only after the contract has been consummated. It is at this point that the indemnitor fully understands his obligation, and—most often—the cost and availability of a method of conveniently handling the risk.

The only sure method for the indifferent to employ is that of carefully reviewing all the provisions of a contract before entering the contract.

For whatever the reason, the party assuming or ceding liability under a contract should make an effort to control the risk which is the result of these contract conditions. Chapter IV is devoted to the methods to be employed in controlling the liability which arises under these circumstances.

CHAPTER II

THE LEGAL PRINCIPLES OF CONTRACTUAL LIABILITY

PUBLIC POLICY TOWARD EXCULPATORY CONTRACTUAL CLAUSES

In general a contract of indemnity—often referred to as a hold harmless agreement—which protects the indemnitee against the consequences of an act which is not a crime or a civil wrong or contrary to public policy is not illegal. These agreements conflict with the common law concept that a man must be responsible for his own wrongs, both to recompense the injured at his (the wrongdoer's) expense and to deter him from further wrongs. Accordingly, the courts appear at times to take upon themselves the responsibility for protecting the unwary, the oppressed and the uninformed where hold harmless clauses come into play. Decisions suggest that many people who execute such agreements do so without knowing their consequences.

Nevertheless, as a general rule, the parties to a contract may lawfully bind themselves to indemnify against or be relieved from liability on account of future acts of negligence, whether the negligence indemnified against be that of the indemnitor or his agents or that of the indemnitee or his agents. The courts are not in accord as to the right of one to limit his liability for his own negligence. On the one extreme, the courts of New Hampshire take the position that no agreement to avoid liability for one's own negligence is enforceable. Other courts take the position that the right to freedom of contract is paramount to the consideration of violation of public policy and will uphold agreements to avoid responsibility for the consequences of one's own negligent act if the intent of the parties is clearly spelled out in the agreement. In all jurisdictions the courts will carefully consider the attempted exculpation to determine whether there is a *viola-*

tion of public policy. A variety of attitudes are expressed as to what constitutes public policy.

It is clear that a contract of indemnity for committing a willful and malicious trespass is illegal and void. There is a conflict of authority as to how far railroads can go in limiting their liability for their own negligence, many courts taking the position that they can limit their liability for negligence as a private carrier but that it is against public policy for them to limit the liability imposed on them by law as a public carrier. In general certain types of indemnity agreements will not be given full effect by the courts where one of the bargaining parties is charged with a public duty, such as a common carrier or public utility, or where the bargaining power of the parties is grossly unequal, but it is not against public policy for one to relieve himself of liability arising from his own negligence.

The validity of an exculpatory provision depends upon a complexity of considerations. The further apart the parties as to their strength of bargaining power and knowledge of the facts, the less likely the agreement will be valid. Conversely the closer the parties come in approaching absolute equality in bargaining strength, the greater the probability that the exculpatory clause will be held valid. It is a general rule that exculpatory clauses are strictly construed by the courts to prevent the liability from being extended beyond the terms of the agreement.

LEGAL BASIS FOR LIABILITY

Liability for Own Actions

All liability is legal or there is no liability. The source may be either tort (civil wrong) or contract (agreement). A person is always responsible for his own torts. Tort liability may be based on intentional misconduct, negligence or strict liability imposed by law. One is liable for intentional injuries he wrongfully inflicts upon another. One is liable if he negligently injures another by failing to exercise the degree of care the law requires of him. One is liable regardless of fault for certain extrahazardous activities such as dynamiting and excavating and where the liability is imposed by law as in workers' compensation cases. As far as the injured party is concerned, the *tort feasor* is liable even though he may have insurance or a hold harmless agreement to shift the ultimate economic burden to another. Contract liability is that imposed by agreement. Again, one is always liable for his contractual undertakings even though he may have insurance or a hold harmless agreement which will shift the ultimate economic burden to another.

Liability for Acts of Agents or Employes

The general rule is that a principal or employer is liable for the acts of his agents or employes which are committed within the scope of the agency or employment. It is not material that the agent or employe failed to follow instructions or in fact violated instructions, so long as the act done was still within the scope of the agency or employment. Where intentional misconduct is involved, the question arises as to whether the actor had left the scope of his agency or employment. Thus, the employer would not be liable when the employe, motivated purely by a personal grudge, gets into a fight and injures a third person. The employer would be liable for the actions of an overzealous employe who assaults a customer in an attempt to collect for his employer. The test is whether the agent or employe, although acting wrongfully and willfully, was nevertheless attempting to further his principal's or employer's business. The principal or employer is liable for actual damages caused by the gross or wanton negligence of his agent or employe but may not be liable for punitive damages which are frequently allowed against a tort feasor for intentional misconduct. The agent or employe, to be sure, is personally liable and is not relieved of liability because his principal or employer is jointly and severally liable along with him for torts committed within the scope of the agency or employment.

Liability for Acts of Independent Contractor

An independent contractor is one who agrees to do a piece of work according to his own judgment and methods. He has the right to employ and direct the action of the workmen independently of the party for whom he is performing, who looks to him only for the end results. That party contracts for the work with no control over the means of its accomplishment. The general rule is that he is not responsible for the torts of the independent contractor. There are, however, some important exceptions. The owner is not relieved from liability if the injury is caused in whole or in part by his own negligence. He may be liable if he knew or by exercise of reasonable care might have learned that the independent contractor was not competent or qualified to do the work. In such a case it would be argued that the owner was negligent in selecting the independent contractor. He would be liable where the work contracted for was illegal or wrongful. Finally, the party who uses an independent contractor may still be liable where the work contracted for is extrahazardous in nature, such as dynamiting and excavating. This rests on the principle that one cannot delegate to another his basic responsibility for such undertakings. The owner is of course always liable where it can be shown that his own negligence caused the loss or injury.

LIABILITY FOR INJURY TO THIRD PERSONS

Sole Negligence of Contractor

Irrespective of whether the party who uses the services of the independent contractor is liable for the negligence of his independent contractor, the contractor himself is liable for his negligence and that of his servants. Thus, if the negligence of an independent contractor causes injury to other contractors or their employes or to the employes of his principal or to his own employes or to some third person for whose protection the contractor is bound to exercise due care, the contractor may be liable for the injury.

Concurrent Negligence of Employer and Independent Contractor

The general rule where the concurrent negligence of two parties causes injury to a third person is that both negligent parties are liable to the third person for the full amount of the injury. Damages are not apportioned in the absence of statute. However, about half the states have statutes providing for contribution in varying circumstances. Furthermore, one who was only under a secondary duty may be entitled to indemnity from the one who was primarily responsible in some situations such as where an employer is held vicariously liable for the tort of a servant or an independent contractor. A number of courts have held that one whose negligence has consisted of mere passive neglect may get contribution from an active wrongdoer although there will be no indemnity in favor of an intentional wrongdoer. It is not possible to give a general rule as to when indemnity will be allowed. It is sometimes based on a duty owed by the indemnitor to the indemnitee, sometimes on the degree of difference in the fault of the two tort feasors, and sometimes on the difference in the duty owed to the injured party. While no one explanation will cover all cases, indemnity between tort feasors is sometimes allowed where it is felt the ends of justice require one tort feasor to indemnify the other.

Shifting Liability by a Contractual Clause

A hold harmless agreement is an agreement between two or more parties defining an obligation or duty resting on one party, the indemnitor, to make good the liability, loss or damage that another party, the indemnitee, has incurred or may incur. In general a party may shift his liability to another party by contract so far as the other party is concerned. The indemnitee would still be liable to injured third parties, but he would then be entitled to indemnity from the indemnitor on the strength of his hold harmless agreement. While the number and types of hold harmless agreements are limited only by the ingenuity of the drafters, the basic types of such agreements are as follows:

1. Party A reaffirms responsibility for *his own negligent acts*. Party B is thus protected in cases where he is held vicariously responsible. He has acquired a *contractual* right to indemnity where the basic tort law of the jurisdiction may or may not entitle him to it.

2. Party A reaffirms responsibility for his own acts and agrees to *share responsibility* for joint and concurrent negligence of both parties. This still leaves the parties basically responsible for their own conduct.

3. Party A assumes responsibility for *all liability* except that arising out of the *sole negligence* of B. Here A assumes all responsibility for concurrent negligence regardless of the degree of fault.

4. Party A assumes responsibility for *all liability without regard to fault*. Here A assumes not only the responsibility for the sole negligence of B, but also the negligence of third parties over whom he has no control.

5. Party A assumes responsibility for all injury, loss or damage to anyone or anything, regardless of fault or cause and *holds B harmless from any claims*. Such agreements would appear to be totally unreasonable,

since they would include even losses over which no one has any control or acts of God. Nevertheless the courts may enforce such agreements which do not violate a statute or public policy, if the intent of the parties is absolutely clear and unequivocal.

Hold harmless agreements will usually be sustained by the courts when the parties clearly express the intent to shift liability and this does not run counter to any statute or public policy. The courts are reluctant to construe contracts to indemnify a person against his own negligence as that would be against public policy, but will do so where the intent is clear from the language and purpose of the agreement.

Hold harmless agreements frequently serve a useful purpose in clarifying the obligations of the parties, in creating a right to indemnity for liability the other party is willing to assume and in protecting a party from vicarious liability imposed by law and for which he might not otherwise have a right to indemnity. The danger is in the unreasonable and promiscuous use of these agreements, imposing liability a party never intended to assume, would not normally bear and in some cases cannot insure himself against.

LIABILITY UNDER WORKERS' COMPENSATION LAWS

General Rule

In general workers' compensation laws require employers to compensate their employes for injuries incurred within the scope of their employment without regard to fault or negligence on the part of the employer. In exchange for this strict liability imposed on the employer, the amount of the recovery from the employer or his insurer is fixed by a predetermined scale or schedule. The employer must either insure this liability or qualify as a self-insurer by establishing financial responsibility.

Subrogation Rights

Where the injury has been caused by a third party tort feasor, the workers' compensation laws vary greatly as to the subrogation rights of the employer or insurer. Generally, but not always, the insurer or employer is subrogated to the claim of the employe against a third party tort feasor to the extent of the compensation paid or awarded. Under some statutes the insurer can sue the tort feasor only for the amount of compensation paid and the employe can sue for the excess damages. Under a few statutes the employe can elect to receive compensation or sue the third party tort feasor for damages. In this arrangement, acceptance of compensation bars further action except by the employer or insurer for the amount of compensation paid. In some states the insurer can collect the full judgment from the tort feasor and will hold the excess over the compensation paid for the employe or his dependents. Generally, the third party is liable for the full amount of the damage he caused whether the suit is by the employe, the employer, the insurer or a combination of these.

Impact of Workers' Compensation Laws

The limited liability of the employer under workers' compensation in a case of serious injuries provides a strong incentive for the injured employe and his attorneys to seek a third party tort feasor, perhaps broadening the concept of negligence in the process. Parties contracting with the employer on the other hand are encouraged to protect themselves with hold harmless agreements. The net result is that the employer or his insurer may wind up bearing the entire economic burder of the loss, rendering the workers' compensation limitation ineffective in fact. Fear of this type of liability in part has caused architects in recent years to limit their liability in construction contracts through the use of hold harmless provisions.

LEGAL BASIS OF DETERMINATION OF
EMPLOYE OR INDEPENDENT CONTRACTOR

One of the more difficult problems confronting anyone attempting to evaluate the significance of a relationship which may involve a hold harmless agreement is the determination of the legal definition of the parties in the relationship. This is especially apparent when questions arise as to whether one of the parties is an employe or is a subcontractor.

The usual business management concern with compliance with both federal and state regulations are directly involved. Some of the regulations which have application are:

> Fair Labor Standards Act
>
> Federal Insurance Contributions Act
>
> Federal Unemployment Act
>
> State Unemployment Acts
>
> State Workers' Compensation Acts

A potential violation of the record-keeping requirements of FLSA is inherent in a situation where an employer treats employes as independent contractors. Similarly, overtime pay requirements and minimum wage provisions may also be violated. An employer can suffer penalties and possible civil and criminal liability for such violations of the FLSA, and from similar lack of compliance with FICA, FUTA and the Internal Revenue Code withholding requirements. Additionally, a lack of compliance with various state unemployment and workers' compensation legislation can lead to liability of the employer if the assumed independent contractors are actually employes.

The distinction between an independent contractor and an employe is an important one, in view of the general rule that an employer or contractee is not liable for the negligence of an independent contractor, but the employer or contractee is liable for the negligence of employes. Accordingly, careful attention should be given to the distinctions which have been made by the courts in separating independent contractor status from servant and employe.

Although it is apparent that there is no absolute rule for determining whether one is an independent contractor or an employe, and that each case must be determined on its own facts, there are a number of factors to consider even though the presence of one or more of these factors in a case is not necessarily conclusive. Such factors are important as guides to the broader question of whether the worker is in fact independent, or subject to the control of the employer, in performing the work. While particular factors and elements are discussed more fully below, it has generally been held that the test of what constitutes independent service lies in the control exercised, the decisive question being who has the right to direct what shall be done and how it shall be done.

The most important test in determining whether a person is an independent contractor or an employe is the control which is reserved by the employer. Independent contractor status depends upon the extent to which the person is in fact independent in performing the work. Broadly stated if the person is under the direct control of the employer, he is an employe; if he is not under such control, he is an independent contractor.

Of course, the employer often reserves a degree of control, to enable verification that the contract is performed according to applicable plans and specifications. The employer may exercise a limited control over the work without rendering the contractor an employe since the relation of employer and employe is not inferable from a mere reservation of powers which do not deprive the contractor of his right to do the work according to his own initiative, in accordance with the contract. The control of the work reserved in the employer which effects an employer-employe relationship is control of the means and manner of performance of the work, as well as of the result; an independent contractor relationship exists where the person doing the work is subject to the will of the employer only as to the result, and not as to the means or manner of accomplishment. However, a person employed to perform certain work is not necessarily an employe because the contract provides that the work shall be subject to the approval or satisfaction of the employer. Such a provision is not an assumption by the employer of the right to control the person employed as to the details or method of doing the work but is merely a provision that the employer may see that the contract is carried out according to the plans and specifications. However, the retention of the right not only to insure compliance with the plans and specifications, but also the retention or exercise of the right to direct the manner in which the work shall be performed, may destroy the independent status of the contractor. It should also be emphasized that it is not the fact of actual interference or exercise of control by the employer, but the existence of the right or authority to interfere or control which renders one an employe rather than an independent contractor.

While it is the right of control, as distinguished from the exercise of control, that is the test for determining whether a person is an employe or an independent contractor, the fact that the employer has actually exercised certain control may be considered as a factor tending to show that he has a right to control. Therefore, it is necessary to examine the evidence not only as to terms of the contract, but also with reference to who actually exercised control of the details of the work, as this tends to prove what the contract really contemplated. In weighing the control exercised, however, authoritative control must be carefully distinguished from a mere suggestion as to particular details as where work furnished is part of a larger undertaking.

Whether a contractor or his employer furnishes the workmen, material, tools and equipment is a factor to be considered in determining whether the contractor is independent, since, as a general rule, employes generally use the means provided by the employer, while independent contractors furnish the labor and materials for doing the work. Thus, evidence to the effect that all the labor required for the performance of the stipulated work was furnished by the contractor, that the contractor hired the persons who assisted him in the performance of the work, that he agreed to furnish all or a portion of the materials required for the performance of the stipulated work is considered indicative of an independent contractor status.

Again, however, whether a contractor or employer furnishes or does not furnish the workmen and material by which certain work is done is not in itself as important as whether the contractor or employer has the power to dictate the particular manner in which the material shall be used and laborers shall do their work. Accordingly, a contractor may be independent, where he has control of the doing of the work, although the employer furnishes and pays certain workmen and furnishes certain appliances and tools for the prosecution of the work.

A retention by the owner of the right to supervise or inspect work as it progresses, for the purpose of determining whether it is completed according to plans and specifications, does not itself operate to create the relation of employer and employe between the owner and those engaged in the work. Thus, an employer of an independent contractor may retain a broad general power of supervision and control as to the *results* of the work so as to insure satisfactory performance of the contract including the right to inspect, to stop the work, to make suggestions or recommendations as to the details of the work, or to prescribe alterations or deviations in the work without changing the relationship from that of owner and independent contractor or the duties arising from that relationship.

Whether the employer or the person employed to do the work has control of the premises on which the work is to be performed is a factor to be considered in determining whether the latter is an independent contractor or an employe, as this factor itself goes to the question of right of control over the work. If the premises on which the work was performed was placed under the control of the person employed, this tends to show that he was an independent contractor. Nor is the relationship of the parties affected by the employer's reservation of a right to enter the premises for the purpose of seeing that the work is performed in accordance with the plans and specifications. Under such circumstances the person employed still remains in possession of the premises, and continues to perform the work under his contract, and not under the direction of the employer.

The measure of compensation for work to be done is sometimes an important element to be considered, but it is not in itself controlling. Thus, the fact that the compensation of a contractor is by the day, in a lump sum, or on a commission basis is not a compelling factory. However, an independent contractor relationship: (1) is probable where the person employed undertakes to perform the work as a whole for a *specific sum*; (2) where the compensation to the person employed is computed with reference to the *quality* of work performed by him; and (3) where compensation to the person employed is to be computed with reference to the amount which he himself is to pay to others for performing the work. Also, it has been held that the factor that remuneration is computed with reference to the time during which a person is engaged in the performance of the work tends to prove that he is not an independent contractor.

The existence of a written contract setting out the payments for work that has been satisfactorily accomplished is often important evidence of independent contractor status. It is helpful if the written document characterizes the parties as independent contractors but the parties' characterization may not control against compelling evidence to the contrary.

Additionally, it is of importance to consider by whom the wages of a contractor's employes are paid, since the circumstance that wages or workmen hired by a contractor are paid by the principal employer tends, in some degree, to show that the contractor is really an employe. But such circumstance is not decisive since its significance is reduced by proof that the wages are paid by the principal employer merely because the contractor is without necessary funds, or because the principal employer desires to protect his property against liens.

The control of workers doing manual labor in the performance of work is an important element in establishing the status of a contractor as independent. The fact that the contractor employs, pays, and has full control over the workers is virtually decisive of his independence. Nor do incidental powers retained, such as the right to compel contractors to discharge workers who are incompetent, necessarily require that the contractors be considered employes. However, where an employer retains the unilateral right to discharge employes of a contractor, such power tends, in some degree, to prove that the contractor is not independent.

The nature of the business or occupation in which a person is engaged may be an important factor to be considered along with others. The fact that work to be done requires special skill for its proper performance tends to show that the relations between the employer and the person employed is an independent one. However, the fact that one is given employment by reason of his special skill does not fix his status as an independent contractor rather than an employe if the employer retains the right to control work, as discussed above.

Persons engaged in certain occupations are generally regarded as independent contractors, as, for example, architects, at least insofar as the preparation of plans is concerned, as opposed to supervision of a building under construction;

24

painters and decorators, vendors, as to vendees in respect of any work which the vendor performs in connection with the contract of sale; bailees; and consignees of goods. Persons in business for themselves are also generally held to be independent contractors, although the contrary view is sometimes taken where their employers exercise considerable control over them.

The power of an employer to terminate a contract or to discharge the person employed at any time, irrespective of whether there is or is not a good cause for so doing, strongly tends to show that the person employed is not an independent contractor but an employe. The relation between the parties is, however, to be determined from all the surrounding factors of control, the sole circumstance that the employer has reserved the right to terminate the work and discharge the contractor does not necessarily make the contractor a mere employe. On the other hand, the fact that the employer cannot terminate the employment strongly tends to show that the contractor is independent.

Contractual provisions authorizing an employer to cancel, forfeit, or revoke a contract under certain specified circumstance have sometimes been seen as tending to show that the person was an employe, although it has been indicated in other cases that such stipulations do not affect the independence of a contract.

In summary, these areas of legal concern for the determination of whether a relationship is that of independent contractor or employe would include the following:

>Right to Control Work
>
>Furnishing of Labor and Materials
>
>Right to Inspect Work
>
>Control of Premises

Compensation

Control of Workers

Nature of Business

Power to Terminate Relationship

These considerations are the most often addressed when a dispute arises on this question. It is obvious that it is not an easy determination and that there is no uniform criterion by which such a judgment can be made. It is also obvious that distinctions do exist between the duties, rights and obligations arising in connection with these relationships, and all factors must be considered in making a final determination as to the status of the party to the contract.

LEGISLATIVE RESTRICTIONS ON HOLD HARMLESS AGREEMENTS

As a result of the efforts of many interested groups, a number of states have enacted legislation which either prohibits, nullifies or modifies hold harmless clauses. Most of these statutes are related to the use of hold harmless agreements in construction contracts. The earlier and more significant bills were passed in Tennessee, California and Washington.

Tennessee Senate Bill 373, effective May 17, 1967, (Tenn. Code Ann. §62-6-123), is representative of the standard or uniform statutory attempt to make void or unenforceable hold harmless agreements used in construction contracts stating as follows:

Section 1. A covenant, promise, agreement or understanding in, or in connection with or collateral to a contract or agreement relative to the construction, alteration, repair or maintenance of a building, structure, appurtenance and appliance, including moving, demolition and excavating connected therewith, purporting to indemnify or hold harmless the promisee against liability for damages arising out of bodily injury to persons or damage to property caused by or resulting from the sole negligence of the promisee, his agents or employes, or indemnitee, is against public policy and is void and unenforceable.

The legislature of Washington passed Senate Bill 464, which was approved April 14, 1967, (Wash. Rev. Code Ann. §4.24.115 [1962 Supp. 1975]), making void and unenforceable hold harmless agreements in construction contracts for acts caused by the sole negligence of the indemnitee as follows:

Section 2. A covenant, promise, agreement or understanding in or in connection with or collateral to, a contract or agreement relative to the construction, alteration, repair, addition to, subtraction from, improvement to, or maintenance of, any building, highway, road, railroad, excavation, or other structure, project, development, or improvement attached to real estate, including moving and demolition in connection therewith, purporting to indemnify against liability for damages arising out of bodily injury to persons or damage to property caused by or resulting from the sole negligence of the indemnitee, his agents or employes is against public policy and is void and unenforceable.

The legislature of California passed Senate Bill 310, approved August 23, 1967, (Calif. Civil Code §2782-84 [West 1974]), making void and unenforceable hold harmless agreements in construction contracts for acts caused by the sole negligence or willful misconduct of the promisee as follows:

§2782. (Public policy invalidating provisions in construction contracts for indemnity against liability based on civil neligence of wilful misconduct of promisee.)

All provisions, clauses, covenants, or agreements contained in, collateral to, or affecting any construction contract and which purport to indemnify the promisee against liability for damages for (a) death or bodily injury to persons, (b) injury to property,

(c) design defects or (d) any other loss, damage or expense arising under either (a), (b), or (c) from the sole negligence or willful misconduct of the promisee or the promisee's agents, servants or independent contractors who are directly responsible to such promisee, are against public policy and are void and unenforceable; provided, however, that this provision shall not affect the validity of any insurance contract, workmen's compensation or agreement issued by an admitted insurer as defined by the Insurance Code: (Added by Stats. 1967, ch. 1327, §1.)

§2782. 1. (Same: Exemption as to responsibility under construction contract.)

Nothing contained in Section 2782 shall prevent a contractor responsible for the performance of a construction contract, as defined in Section 2783, from indemnifying fully a person, firm, corporation, state or other agency for whose account the construction contract is not being performanced but who, as an accommodation, enters into an agreement with the contractor permitting such contractor to enter upon or adjacent to its property for the purpose of performing such construction contracts for others. (Added by Stats. 1968, ch. 44, §1.)

§2782.5. Allocation or limitation of liability as between parties for design defects.

Nothing contained in Section 2782 shall prevent a party to a construction contract and the owner or other party for whose account the construction contract is being performed, from agreeing with respect to the allocation or limitation as between the parties of any liability for design defects. (Added by Stats. 1967, ch. 1327, §2.)

§2783. ("Construction contract.")

As used in Sections 2782 and 2782.5, "construction contract" is defined as any agreement or understanding, written or oral, respecting the construction, surveying, design, specifications, alteration, repair, improvement, maintenance, removal of or demolition of any building, highway, road, parking facility, bridge, railroad, airport, pier or dock, excavation or other structure, development or other improvement to real or personal property, or an agreement to perform any portion thereof or any act collateral thereto, or to perform any service reasonably related thereto, including, but not limited to, the erection of all structures or performance of work in connection therewith, the rental of all equipment, all incidental transportation, crane and rigging service and other goods and services furnished in connection therewith. (Added by Stats. 1967, ch. 1327, §3.)

§2784. ("Design defect.")

As used in Sections 2782 and 2782.5, a "design defect" is defined as a condition arising out of its design which renders a structure, item of equipment or machinery or any other similar object, movable or immovable, when constructed substantially in accordance with its design, inherently unfit, either wholly or in part, for its intended use or which impairs or renders the use of such structure, equipment, machinery or property dangerous. (Added by Stats. 1967, ch. 1327, §4.)

§2784.5 (Trucking or cartage contract protecting promisee from liability based on sole negligence or willful misconduct: Exception.)

Any provision, promise, agreement, clause, or covenant contained in, collateral to, or affecting any hauling, trucking or cartage contract or agreement in against public policy void and unenforceable if it purports to indemnify the promisee against liability for any of the following damages which are caused by the sole negligence or willful misconduct of the promisee, agents, servants; or the independent contractors directly responsible to the promisee, except when such agents, servants, or independent contractors are under the direct supervision and control of the promisor:

(a) Damages arising out of bodily injury or death to persons.

(b) Damage to property.

(c) Any other damage or expense arising under either (a) or (b).

This section shall not affect the validity of any insurance contract, workmen's compensation insurance contract, or agreement issued by an admitted insurer as defined by Sections 23 and 24 of

> the Insurance Code or insurance effected by surplus line brokers
> under Sections 1760 through 1780 of the Insurance Code.
> (Added by Stats. 1967, ch. 1314, §1.)

The question would arise as to whether the California legislation would prevent the shifting of liability through a hold harmless agreement where the indemnitor had purchased appropriate contractual liability insurance, since this provision does not affect the validity of any insurance contract and this matter would remain open for construction by the courts. Apparently as to design defects, the parties may shift liability as between themselves for sole negligence or willful misconduct but cannot effectively shift liability to another party for third party claims.

These three earlier statutes, though varying considerably in scope and application, can be summarized as "standard" forms. The Tennessee bill seems to be the more direct application to the restriction of transfer of liability in construction contracts.

The summary which follows is in alphabetical order, by state, indicating the current status of legislative efforts in this area. Neither the statutes themselves nor the comments relating thereto should be used as authoritative commentary. One should thoroughly research the legal areas in one's own jurisdiction before making a judgment on the subject.

STATE STATUTES AND RELEVANT CASE LAW

ALASKA

> §45.45.900. Indemnification agreements contra to public policy.
> A provision clause, covenant, or agreement contained in, collateral to, or affecting any construction contract which purports

to indemnify the promisee against liability for damages for (1) death or bodily injury to persons, (2) injury to property, (3) design defects, or (4) any other loss, damage or expense arising under (1), (2), or (3) of this section from the sole negligence or willful misconduct of the promisee or the promisee's agents, servants or independent contractors who are directly responsible to the promisee, is against public policy and is void and unenforceable; however, this provision does not affect the validity of any insurance contract, workers' compensation or agreement issued by an insurer subject to the provisions of AS21. (§1 ch 155 SLA 1975; am § 60 ch 94 SLA 1980)

COMMENT:

This section became effective on September 23, 1975, and governs contracts executed on or after the date. Contracts executed before that date are governed by the rule announced in *Burgess Construction Co. v. State,* 619 P.2d 1380 (1980), that an indemnity clause is effective to shift responsibility for an accident where the idemnitee is negligent and the indemnitor is not. *Stephen & Sons v. Municipality of Anchorage,* Sup. Ct. Op. No. 2368 (File No. 5102), 629 P.2d 71 (1981).

ARIZONA

§34-226. Indemnity agreements in construction and architect-engineer contracts void; definition

A. A covenant, clause or understanding in, collateral to or affecting a construction contract or architect-engineer professional service contract which purports to indemnify or hold harmless the promisee against liability for loss or damage resulting from the sole negligence of the promisee, his agents, employees or indemnitee is void.

B. Nothing contained in this section shall prevent a contractor responsible for the performance of a construction contract

31

from fully indemnnifying a person, firm corporation, state or other agency for whose account the construction contract is not being performed but who, as an accomodation, enters into an agreement with the contractor permitting such contractor to enter upon or adjacent to its property for the purpose of performing such construction contract for others.

C.   In this section "architect-engineer contract" means a written or oral agreement relating to the design of any construction, alteration, repair, maintenance, moving, demolition or excavation of a structure, highway, appurtenance or other development or improvement to land.

D.   In this section "construction contract" means a written or oral agreement relating to the construction, alteration, repair, maintenance, moving, demolition or excavation of a structure, highway, appurtenance or other development or improvement to land.

COMMENT:

This section makes void hold harmless agreements in construction and design contracts which attempt to indemnify the indemnitee for its sole negligence. Refer to *Estes Co. v. Aztec Construction, Inc.* (App. 1983) 139 Ariz. 166, 677 P. 2d 939.

CONNECTICUT

§52-572K. Hold harmless clause against public policy in certain construction contracts

(a)   Any covenant, promise, agreement or understanding entered into in connection with or collateral to a contract or agreement relative to the construction, alteration, repair or maintenance of any building, structure or appurtenances thereto including moving, demolition and excavating connected therewith, that purports to indemnify or hold harmless the promisee against liability for damage arising out of bodily injury to persons or damage to property caused by or resulting from the sole negligence of such promisee, his agents or employees, is against public policy and void, provided this section shall not affect the validity of any insurance contract, workers' compensation agreement or other agreement issued by a licensed insurer.

(b) The provisions of this section shall apply to covenants, promises, agreements or understanding entered into on or after the thirtieth day next succeeding October 1, 1977.

COMMENT:

The legislature in specifically outlawing hold harmless agreements in the construction industry showed intention that such practice was not to be deemed against public policy in other situations, and clause in vehicle lease by which lessee agreed to indemnify and hold lessor harmless from any and all liability, encompassing promise to indemnify even neglient indemnitee, was not contrary to public policy. *Burkle v. Car and Truck Leasing Co., Inc.,* 467 A.2d 1255 (1983), 1 Conn. App.54.

DELAWARE

§2704. Exculpatory clauses in certain contracts void.

(a) A covenant, promise, agreement or understanding in, or in connection with or collateral to, a contract or agreement (including but not limited to a contract or agreement with the State, any county, municipality or political subdivision of the State, or with any agency, commission, department, body or board of any of them, as well as any contract or agreement with a private party or entity) relative to the construction, alteration, repair or maintenance of a road, highway.

COMMENT:

1. The purpose of this section is to prevent owners and their affiliated preconstruction professional people who furnish plans, designs and specifications from contracting away their duty to stand behind their product. *Martindale v. Getty Ref. & Marketing Co.*, 510 F. Supp. 188 (D. Del. 1981).

2. This section has been determined to apply only to agreements covering preconstruction matters and is not applicable to a refinery maintenance agreement. *James v. Getty Oil Co.*, Del. Super., 472 A.2d 33 (1983).

3. This section does not invalidate exculpatory clause in maintenance contract between owner of construction and contractor whereby the contractor agrees to indemnify the owner for any personal injuries arising out of the owner's negligence, where the owner was not involved in the planning or preconstruction phase of the maintenance work performed by the contractor. *Martindale v. Getty Ref. & Marketing Co.*, 510 F.Supp.188 (D.Del. 1981).

FLORIDA

§725.06. Any portion of any agreement or contract for, or in connection with, any construction, alteration, repair, or demolition of a building, structure, appurtenance, or appliance, including moving and excavating connected with it, or any guarantee of, or in connection with, any of them, between an owner of real property and an architect, engineer, general contractor, subcontractor, or materialman, or between any combination thereof, wherein any party referred to herein obtains indemnification from liability for damages to persons or property caused in whole or in part by any act, omission, or default of that party arising from the contract or its performance shall be void and unenforceable unless:

(1) The contract contains a monetary limitation on the extent of the indemnification and shall be a part of the project specifications or bid documents, if any, or

(2) The person indemnified by the contract gives a specific consideration to the indemnitor for the indemnification that shall be provided for in his contract and section of the project specifications or bid documents if any.

COMMENT:

This statute allows only comparative fault indemnification unless there is (a) a monetary limitation of the extent of the indemnification or (b) specific consideration for the indemnification is provided by the indemnitee in the contract.

GEORGIA

13-8-2. Contracts contravening public policy generally.

(a) A contract which is against the policy of the law cannot be enforced. Contracts deemed contrary to public policy include but are not limited to:

(1) Contracts tending to corrupt legislation or the judiciary;

(2) Contracts in general restraint in trade;

(3) Contracts to evade or oppose the revenue laws of another country;

(4) Wagering contracts;

(5) Contracts of maintenance or champerty.

(b)   A covenant, promise, agreement, or understanding in or in connection with or collateral to a contract or agreement relative to the construction, alteration, repair, or maintenance of a building, structure, appurtenances, and appliances including moving, demolition, and excavating connected therewith, purporting to indemnify or hold harmless the promisee against liability for damages arising out of bodily injury to persons or damage to property caused by or resulting from the sole negligence of the promisee, his agents or employees, or indemnitee is against public policy and is void and unenforceable, provided that this subsection shall not affect the validity of any insurance contract, workers' compensation, or agreement issued by an admitted insurer. (Orig. Code 1863, § 2714, Code 1868, § 2708; Code 1873, § 2750; Code 1882, § 2750; Civil Code 1895, § .3668; Civil Code 1910, 253; Code 1933, § 20-504; Ga. L. 1970, p. 441, § 1; Ga. L. 1982, p. 3. § 13.)

COMMENT:

1.   Contracts of express indemnity are construed strictly and, absent plain, clear, and unequivocal language, will not be interpreted to indemnify against acts attributable to indemnitee's own negligence. *Binswanger Glass Co. v. Beers Constr. Co.*, 141 Ga. App. 715, 234 S.E.2d 363 (1977).

2.   A landlord's implied warranty concerning latent defects existing at inception of lease is sufficiently analagous to a contract for maintenance or repair that an exculpatory provision purporting to nullify the effect of such implied warranty is void and unenforceable under subsection (b) of this section. *Country Club Apts., Inc. v. Scott,* 154 Ga. App. 217, 267 S.E.2d 811 (1980); *Porubiansky v. Emory Univ.*, 156 Ga. App. 602, 275 S.E.2d 163 (1980).

3.   Purpose of subsection (b) of this section is to prevent a building contractor, subcontractor, or owner from contracting away liability for accidents caused solely by his

36

negligence, whether during the construction of the building or after the structure is completed and occupied. *Smith v. Seaboard C.L.R.R.*, 639 F.2d 1235 (5th Cir 1981).

HAWAII

§431-453 Construction industry; indemnity agreements invalid. Any covenant, promise, agreement or understanding in, or in connection with or collateral to, a contract or agreement relative to the construction, alteration, repair, or maintenance of a building, structure, appurtenance or appliance, including moving, demolition, or excavating connected therewith, purporting to indemnify the promisee against liability for bodily injury to persons or damage to property caused by or resulting from the sole negligence of the promisee, his agents or employees, or indemnitee is invalid as against public policy, and is void and unenforceable; provided that this section shall not affect any valid workers' compensation claim under chapter 386 or any other insurance contract or agreement issued by an admitted insurer upon any insurable interest under this chapter. (L 1970, c 169, §2; am L 1975, c 41, §1]

COMMENT:

Statute invalidates broad form hold harmless clauses in construction contracts which attempt to transfer liability for the indemnitee's sole negligence or willful misconduct.

IDAHO

§29-114. Indemnification of promisee for negligence — Effect on existing agreements.

(a) A covenant, promise, agreement or understanding in, or in connection with or collateral to, a contract or agreement relative to the construction, alteration, repair or

37

maintenance of a building, structure, highway, appurtenance and appliance, including moving, demolition and excavating connected therewith, purporting to indemnify the promisee against liability for damages arising out of bodily injury to persons or damage to property caused by or resulting from the sole negligence of the promisee, his agents or employees, or indemnitees, is against public policy and is void and unenforceable.

This act will not be construed to affect or impair the obligations of contracts or agreements, which are in existence at the time the act becomes effective (May 18, 1971). (1971, ch. 46, *z8* 1, p. 100).

COMMENT:

This statute makes void broad form indemnity clauses in construction contracts which attempt to indemnify the indemnitee for its sole negligence. Refer to *Steiner Corp. v. Commercial Dist. Tel.*, - Idaho 683 P.2d 435 (1984).

ILLINOIS

29 §61. Indemnification of person from person's own negligence - Effect - Enforcement.

§1. With respect to contracts or agreements, either public or private, for the construction of, or for any moving, demolition or excavation connected therewith, every convenant, promise or agreement to indemnify or hold harmless another person from that person's own negligence is void as against public policy and wholly unenforceable.

COMMENT:

1.   Under Illinois law, exculpatory clauses will not be enforced between certain parties where public interest in rela-

tionship or disparity in bargaining power exists. *Gates Rubber Co. v. USM Corp.*, C.A. 1975, 508 F.2d 603.

2. Where lessor provided not only 90-ton capacity mobile crane to be used in dismantling and moving to tower crane, but also provided the operator for the mobile crane, lessor became a subcontractor in the construction of a building and the provision of the lease agreement which indemnified the lessor from its own negligence was voided by this paragraph. *American Pecco Corp. v. Concrete Bldg. Systems Co.*, D.C. Ill., 392 F.Supp. 789.

3. Clause in subcontract purporting to require subcontractor to indemnify and save harmless the general contractor from liability arising out of injuries or death or property damage caused by violation of the Structural Work Act (ch. 48, par. 60 et seq.) was void as against public policy and unenforceable. *Pilon v. George A. Johnson & Son*, App. 3 Dist. 1984, 80 Ill. Dec. 908, 125 Ill. App. 3d 587, 466 N.E. 2d 360.

INDIANA

26-2-5-1. Agreements of indemnification void - Exception. -

All provisions, clauses, covenants, or agreements contained in, collateral to, or affecting any construction or design contract except those pertaining to highway contracts, which purport to indemnify the promisee against liability for:

(1)   death or bodily injury to persons;

(2)   injury to property;

(3)   design defects; or

39

(4) any other loss, damage or expense arising under either (1), (2) or (3); from the sole negligence or willful misconduct of the promisee or the promisee's agents, servants or independent contractors who are directly responsible to the promisee, are against public policy and are void and unenforceable. [IC 1971, 26-2-5-1, as added by Acts 1975, P.L. 276, § 1, p. 1524.]

COMMENT:

A "construction contract" involves hazardous construction work requiring safe working conditions and ultimately a safe product, and "construction work" means to build, erect, or create. *Ogilvie v. Steele*, - Ind. App. -, 452 N.E. 2d 167 (1983).

LOUISIANA

R.S. 38:2216(D) Written Contract and Bond

D. It is hereby declared that any provision contained in a public contract, other than contract of insurance, providing for a hold harmless or indemnity agreement, or both, from the contractor to the public body for damage arising out of injuries or property damage to third parties caused by the negligence of the public body, its employees or agents are contrary to the public policy of the state of Louisiana, and any and all such provisions in any and all public contracts issued after the effective date hereof, are null and void.

R.S. 9: Certain Indemnification Agreements Invalid

A. The legislature finds that an inequity is foisted on certain contractors and their employees by the defense or indemnity provisions either or both, contained in some agreements pertaining to wells for oil, gas, or water, or drilling for minerals which occur in a solid, liquid, gaseous, or other state, to the extent those provisions apply to death or bodi-

40

ly injury to persons. It is the intent of the legislature by this Section to declare null and void and against public policy of the state of Louisiana any provision in any agreement which requires defense and/or indemnification for death or bodily injury to persons, where there is negligence or fault (strict liability) on part of the indemnitee, or an agent or employee of the indemnitee, or an independent contractor who is directly responsible to the indemnitee.

B. Any provision contained in, collateral to, or affecting an agreement pertaining to a well for oil, gas or water, or drilling for minerals which occur in a solid, liquid, gaseous, or other state, is void and unenforceable to the extent that it purports to or does provide for defense or indemnity, or either, to the indemnitee against loss or liability for damages arising out of or resulting from death or bodily injury to persons, which is caused by or results from the sole or concurrent negligence or fault (strict liability) of the indemnitee, or an agent, employee, or an independent contractor who is directly responsible to the indemnittee.

COMMENT:

Two statutes apply in Louisiana. The first renders null and void hold harmless clauses in public contracts which seek to indemnify the public body for its own negligence. The second statute allows comparative fault indemnification of the indemnitee in oil, gas, water or mineral drilling contracts.

MARYLAND

§5-305. Certain construction industry indemnity agreements prohibited.

A covenant, promise, agreement or understanding in, or in connection with or collateral to, a contract or agreement relating to the construction, alteration, repair or maintenance of a building, structure, appurtenance or appliance, including moving demolition and excavating connected with it, purporting to indemnify the promisee against liability for damages arising out of bodily injury to any person or damage to property caused by or resulting from the sole negligence of the promisee or indemnitee, his agents or employees, is against public policy and is void and unenforceable. This section does not affect the validity of any insurance contract, workmen's compensation, or any other agreement issued by an insurer. (1974, ch. 634; 1975, ch. 87.)

COMMENT:

A contract which did not purport to indemnify the promisee for damages resulting from its sole negligence is beyond the prescription of this section. *Scarborough v. Ridgeway*, 726 F.2d 132 (4th Cir.1984).

MICHIGAN

§691-991. Building industry; certain contracts for indemnification void.

Section 1. A covenant, promise, agreement or understanding in, or in connection with or collateral to, a contract or agreement relative to the construction, alteration, repair or maintenance of a building, structure, appurtenance and appliance, including moving demolition and excavating connected therewith, purporting to indemnify the promisee against liability for damages arising out of bodily injury to persons or damage to property caused by or resulting from the sole negligence of the promisee or indemnity, his agents or employees, is against public policy and is void and unenforceable. P.A.1966, No. 165, § 1, Eff. March 10, 1967.

COMMENT:

Language of indemnity contract providing for indemnification of a general contractor for any and all suits to

42

which the general contractor contributed in whole or in part was insufficient, by itself, to indicate an intention to indemnify the general contractor for its own negligence and, thus, the contract was not void as against public policy. *Harbenski v. Upper Peninsula Power Co.*, 325 N.W.2d 785 (1982), 118 Mich.App. 440.

MINNESOTA

§337.01. Building and construction contracts; indemnification agreements.

Subdivision 1. Definition. As used in sections 337.01 to 337.05 the following terms have the meanings assigned to them.

Subdivision 2. Building and construction contract. "building and construction contract" means a contract for the design, construction, alteration, improvement, repair or maintenance of real property, highways, roads or bridges. The term does not include contracts for the maintenance or repair of machinery, equipment or other such devices used as part of a manufacturing, converting or other production process, including electric, gas, steam, and telephone utility equipment used for production, transmission, or distribution purposes.

Subdivision 3. Indemnification agreement. "Indemnification agreement" means an agreement by the promisor to indemnify or hold harmless the promisee against liability or claims of liability for damages arising out of bodily injury to persons or out of physical damage to tangible or real property.

Subdivision 4. Promisee. "Promisee" includes that party's independent contractors, agents, employees or indemnitees.

§337.02 Unenforceability of certain agreements

An indemnification agreement contained in, or executed in connection with, a building and construction contract is unenforceable except to the extent that the underlying injury or damage is attributable to the negligence or otherwise wrongful act or omission, including breach of a specific contractual duty of the promisor or the promisor's independent contractors, agents, employees, or delegates.

337.03. Nonapplication to certain agreements

Sections 337.01 to 337.05 do not apply to an agreement by which a promisor that is a party to a building and construction contract indemnifies a person, firm, corporation, or public agency for whose account the construction is not being performed, but who, as an accommodation, permits the promisor or the promisor's independent contractors, agents, employees, or delegates to enter upon or adjacent to its property for the purpose of performing the building and construction contract. Sections 337.01 to 337.05 do not apply to an indemnification agreement that is an integral part of an offer to compromise or settlement of a disputed claim, if:

(a)   the settlement is based on consideration;

(b)   The dispute relates to an alleged event that is related to a construction contract and that occurred before the settlement is made; and

(c)   the indemnification relates only to claims that have arisen or may arise from the past event.

337.04 Validity of other agreements

Section 337.01 to 337.05 do not affect the validity of any insurance contract, workers' compensation agreement, construction bond, or other agreement lawfully issued by an insurer or bonding company.

337.05 Agreements to insure

Subdivision 1. Agreements valid. Sections 337.01 to 337.05 do not affect the validity of agreements whereby a promisor agrees to provide specific insurance coverage for the benefit of others.

Subdivision 2. Indemnification for breach of agreement. If:

(a)   a promisor agrees to provide specific types and limits of insurance; and

(b)   a claim arises within the scope of the specified insurance; and

(c)   The promisor did not obtain and keep in force the specified insurance;

then, as to that claim and regardless of section 337.02, the promisee shall have indemnification from the promisor to the same extent as the specified insurance.

Subdivision 3. When indemnification not available. The indemnification stated in subdivision 2 is not available if:

(a)   the specified insurance was not reasonably available in the market; and

(b)   the promisor so informed the other party to the agreement to insure before signing the agreement, or signed the agreement subject to a written exception as to the nonavailable insurance.

Subdivision 4. Indemnification regarding deductible amounts. If:

(1)   a promisor agrees to provide specific types and limits of insurance; and

(2)   a claim arises within the scope of the specified insurance; and

(3)   the insurance provided by the promisor includes a self-insured retention or a deductible amount;

then, as to that claim and regardless of section 337.02, the promises shall have indemnification from the promisor to the full extent of the deductible amount or self-insured retention.

45

Subdivision 5. No waiver by certificates. A promisor's obligation to provide specified insurance is not waived by either or both of the following:

(1)   a promisee's failure to require or insist upon certificates or other evidence of insurance;

(2)   a promisee's acceptance of a certificate or other evidence of insurance that shows a variance from the specified coverage.

COMMENT:

The Minnesota Statutes permit only limited comparative fault indemnification agreements in construction contracts but does not prevent the indemnitor from agreeing to provide insurance coverage for the indemnitee's negligence. If the indemnitor agrees, and fails to procure the insurance, the indemnitee is entitled to indemnification to the same limits as required in the insurance specifications.

MISSISSIPPI

31-5-41. "Hold harmless" clauses in construction are void; exceptions.

With respect to all public or private contracts or agreements, for the construction, alteration, repair or maintenance of buildings, structures, highway bridges, viaducts, water sewer or gas distribution systems, or other work dealing with construction, or for any moving, demolition or excavation connected therewith, every covenant, promise and/or agreement contained therein to indemnify or hold harmless another person from that person's own negligence is void as against public policy and wholly unenforceable.

This section does not apply to construction bonds or insurance contracts or agreements.

COMMENT:

A contractual provision indemnifying defendant tire company from liability arising out of performance of work on its premises by a painting company was ineffective, in light of this statute, to shield defendant from liability to a paint company employee who was burned in a fire while painting on defendant's premises and who alleged that defendant had provided an unsafe work place. No exception from the statute was available for parties of equal bargaining strength. There was no provision for contribution to the settlement burden by the painting company. Subsection (b) of the statute, exempting insurance contracts, was not applicable since the contract at issue was an insured indemnity contract. And neither implied indemnity nor quasi contractual indemnity was available. *Crosby v. General Tire & Rubber Co.* (CA5 Ala) 543 F2d 1128.

NEBRASKA

25-1153. Contract or agreement; indemnity provisions; against public policy; unenforceable; when. In the event that a public or private contract or agreement, for the construction, alteration, repair, or maintenance of a building, structure, highway bridge, viaduct, water, sewer, or gas distribution system or other work dealing with construction, or for any moving, demolition, or excavation connected with such construction, contains a covenant, promise, agreement, or combination thereof, to indemnify or hold harmless another person from that person's own negligence, then such covenant, promise, agreement, or combination thereof is void as against public policy and wholly unenforceable.

This section shall not apply to construction bonds or insurance contracts, or agreements.

COMMENT:

This statute disallows broad form and intermediate form indemnity agreements in construction contracts. Refer to *Omaha Bank for Cooperatives v. the Aetna Casualty and Surety Company*, No. 42981. Supreme Court of Nebraska, 1982.

NEW HAMPSHIRE

338-A:1. Indemnification Agreements Prohibited. Any agreement or provision whereby an architect, engineer, surveyor or his agents or employees is sought to be held harmless or indemnified for damages and claims arising out of circumstances giving rise to legal liability by reason of negligence on the part of any said persons shall be against public policy, void and wholly unenforceable.

COMMENT:

This statute disallows broad form and intermediate form hold harmless clauses when the indemnitee is an architect, engineer or surveyor. Refer to *Hamilton v. Volkswagen of America, Inc.*, No. 83-320, Supreme Court of New Hampshire, 1984.

NEW JERSEY

2A:40A-1. Construction, alteration, repair, maintenance, servicing or security of building, highway, railroad, appurtenance and appliance; invalidity.

A covenant, promise, agreement or understanding in, or in connection with or collateral to a contract, agreement or purchase order, relative to the construction, alteration, repair, maintenance, servicing, or security of a building, structure, highway, railroad, appurtenance and appliance, including moving, demolition, excavating, grading, clearing, site preparation or development of real property connected therewith, purporting to indemnify or hold harmless the promisee against liability for damages arising out of bodily injury to persons or damage to property *caused by or resulting from the sole negligence of the promisee, his agents, or employees*, is against public policy and is void and unenforceable; provided that this section shall not affect the validity of any insurance contract, workmen's compensation or agreement issued by an authorized insurer.

L.1981, c.317, § 1, eff. Dec. 3, 1981. Amended by L.1983, c. 107 § 1, eff. March 14, 1983.

2A:40A-2. Architect, engineer, surveyor of agents for damages, claims, losses or expenses arising out of preparation or approval of maps, opinions, change orders, designs or specifications, or giving of or failure to give directions or instructions; invalidity.

A covenant, promise, agreement or understanding in, or in connection with or collateral to a contract, agreement or purchase order, whereby an architect, engineer, surveyor or his agents, servants or employees shall be indemnified or held harmless for damages, claims, losses or expenses including attorneys; fees *caused by or resulting from the sole negligence of an engineer, surveyor of his agents, servants, or employees and* arising either out of (1) the preparation or approval by an architect, engineer, surveyor or his agents, servants, employees or invitees, of maps, drawings, opinions, reports, surveys, change orders, designs or specifications, (2) or giving of or failure to give directions or instructions by the architect, engineer, surveyor or his agents, servants, or employees; provided such giving or failure to give is the cause of the damage, claim, loss or expense, is against public policy and is void and unenforceable.

L.1981, c.317, § 2, eff. Dec. 3, 1981. Amended by L.1983, c. 107 § 2, eff. March 14, 1983.

COMMENT:

This statute voids all hold harmless clauses in (a) construction contracts and (b) contracts where the indemnitee is an architect, engineer or surveyor, and the bodily injury or property damage arises out of design or supervision.

NEW MEXICO

56-7-1. [Real property; negligence, acts or omissions of indemnitee; certain agreements void.]

Any provision contained in any agreement relating to the construction, installation, alteration, modification, repair, maintenance, servicing, demolition, excavation, drilling, reworking, grading, paving, clearing, site preparation or development, of any real property, or any improvement of any kind whether on, above or under real property, including without limitation, building, shafts, wells and structures, by which any party to the agreement agrees to indemnify the indemnitee, or the agents and the employees of the indemnitee, against liability, claims, damages, losses or expenses, including attorney fees, arising out of bodily injury to persons or damage to property caused by, or resulting from, in whole or in part, the negligence, act or omission of the indemnitee, or the agents of employees of the indemnitee, or any legal entity for whose negligence, acts or omissions any of them may be liable, is against public policy and is void and unenforceable, unless such provision shall provide that the agreement to indemnify shall not extend to liability, claims, damages, losses or expenses, including attorney fees, arising out of:

A. the preparation or approval of maps, drawings, opinions, reports, surveys, change orders, designs or specifications by the indemnitee, or the agents or employees of the indemnitee; or

B. The giving of or the failure to give directions or instructions by the indemnitee, or the agents or employees of the indemnitee, where such giving or failure to give directions or instructions is the primary cause of bodily injury to persons or damage to property.

The word "indemnify" as used in this section includes, without limitation, an agreement to remedy damage or loss caused in whole or part by the negligence, act or omission of the indemnitee, the agents or employees of the indemnitee, or any legal entity for whose negligence, acts or omissions any of the foregoing may be liable.

56-7-2. Agreements, covenants and promises to indemnify void.

A. Any agreement, covenant or promise contained in, collateral to or affecting any agreement pertaining to any well for oil, gas or water, or mine for any mineral, which purports to indemnify the indemnitee against loss or liability for damages, for:

(1) death or bodily injury to persons; or

(2) injury to property; or

(3) any other loss, damage or expense arising under either Paragraph (1) and (2) or both; or

(4) any combination of these, arising from the sole or concurrent negligence of the indemnitee or the agents or employees of the indemnitee or any independent contractor who is directly responsible to the indemnitee, or from any accident which occurs in operations carried on at the direction or under the supervision of the indemnitee or an employee or representative of the indemnitee or in accordance with methods and means specified by the indemnitee or employees or representatives of the indemnitee, is against public policy and is void and unenforceable. This provision shall not affect the validity of any insurance contract or any benefit conferred by the Workmen's Compensation Act [52-1-1 to 52-1-69 NMSA 1978].

B. As used in this section, "agreement pertaining to any well for oil, gas or water, or mine for any mineral" means any agree-

51

ment or understanding, written or oral, concerning any operations related to drilling, deepening, reworking, repairing, improving, testing, treating, perforating, acidizing, logging, conditioning, altering, plugging or otherwise rendering services in, or in connection with, any well drilled for the purpose of producing or disposing of oil, gas or other minerals or water, and designing, excavating, constructing, improving or otherwise rendering services on, or in connection with, any mine shaft, drift or other structure intended for use in the exploration of, or production of, any mineral, or an agreement to perform any portion of any such work or services or any act collateral thereto, including the furnishing or rental of equipment, incidental transportation and other goods and services furnished in connection with any such service or operation.

C.   Nothing in this section shall deprive an owner of the surface estate of the right to secure an indemnity from any lessee, operator, contractor or other person conducting operations for the exploration or production of minerals of the owners' land.

COMMENT:

1.   Tenant's agreement to indemnify landlord against all claims as including losses resulting from landlord's negligence, 4 A.L.R. 4th 798.

2.   Indemnitee cannot contract away liability for own negligence. The language in subsection A(4) which makes void and unenforceable any agreement which purports to indemify an indemnitee for injuries or death "arising from the . . . concurrent negligence of the indemnitee" means only the indemnitee cannot contract away liability for his own percentage of negligence. *Guitard v. Gulf oil Co.*, 100 N.M. 358, 670 P.2d 969 (Ct. App. 1983).

NEW YORK

5-322.1. Agreements exempting owners and contractors from liability for negligence void and unenforceable; certain cases.

1. A covenant, promise, agreement or understanding in, or in connection with or collateral to a contract or agreement relative to the construction, repair or maintenance of a building, structure, appurtenances and appliances including moving, demolition and excavating connected therewith, purporting to indemnify or hold harmless the promisee against liability for damage arising out of bodily injury to persons or damage to property contributed to, caused by or resulting from the negligence of the promisee, his agents or employees, or indemnitee, whether such negligence be in whole or in part, is against public policy and is void and unenforceable; provided that this section shall not affect the validity of any insurance contract, workers' compensation agreement or other agreement issued by an admitted insurer. This subdivision shall not preclude a promise requiring indemnification for damages arising out of bodily injury to persons or damage to property caused by or resulting from the negligence of a party other than the promisee, whether or not the promisee is partially negligent.

COMMENT:

Clause in building maintenance contract requiring contractor to indemnify city, building owner, for all liability arising out of or in connection with the contract was enforceable where personal injuries caused by negligence in maintenance of a boiler was not caused by or resulted from the sole negligence of the city. *Quevedo v. City of New York,* 1982, 56 N.Y.2d 150, 451 N.Y.S.2d 651, 436 N.E.2d 1253, reargument denied 57 N.Y.2d 674, 454 N.Y.S.2d 1032, 439 N.E.2d 1247.

NORTH CAROLINA

22B-1. Construction indemnity agreements invalid.

Any promise or agreement in, or in connection with a contract or agreement relative to the design, planning, construction, alteration, repair or maintenance of a building, structure, highway, road, appurtenance or appliance, including moving, demolition and excavating connected therewith, purporting to indemnify or hold harmless the promisee, the promisee's independent contractors, agents, employees, or indemnitees against liability for damages arising out of bodily injury to persons or damage to property proximately caused by or resulting from the negligence, in whole or in part, of the promisee, its independent contractors, agents, employees, or indemnitees, is against public policy and is void and unenforceable. Nothing contained in this section shall prevent or prohibit a contract, promise or agreement whereby a promisor shall indemnify or hold harmless any promisee or the promisee's independent contractors, agents, employees or indemnitees against liability for damages resulting from the sole negligence of the promisor, its agents or employees. This section shall not affect an insurance contract, workmen's compensation, or any other agreement issued by an insuror, nor shall this section apply to promises or agreements under which a public utility as defined in G.S. 62-3(23) including a railroad corporation as an indemnitee. This section shall not apply to contracts entered into by the Department of Transportation pursuant to G.S. 136-28.1 (1079, c./ 57, s.1.)

COMMENT:

This statute allows only limited comparative fault indemnification clauses in construction contracts. This statute does not affect insurance contracts or agreements under which the indemnitee is a public utility, railroad or the North Carolina Department of Transportation. Refer to *Lewis v. Dunn Leasing Corp.and John Willis* No. 7718SC412. Court of Appeals of North Carolina, 1978.

NORTH DAKOTA

9-08-02.1 Contracts against liabiity for errors or omissions - Void.

Any provision in a construction contract which would make the contractor liable for the errors or omissions of the owner or his agents in the plans and specifications of such contract is against public policy and void.

COMMENT:

A stipulation not to be held responsible for any acts or torts in the future is against public policy. *Roll v. Keller*, 336 NW 2d 648 (1983).

OHIO

2305.31. [Indemnify promisee against damage liability.]

A covenant, promise, agreement or understanding in, or in connection with or collateral to, a contract or agreement relative to the construction, alteration, repair or maintenance of a building, structure, highway, road, appurtenance and appliance, including moving, demolition and excavating connected therewith, pursuant to which contract or agreement the promisee, or its independent contractors, agents or employees has hired the promisor to perform work, purporting to indemnify the promisee, its independent contractors, agents, employees, or indemnities against liability for damages arising out of bodily injury to persons or damage to property initiated or proximately caused by or resulting from the negligence of the promisee, its independent contractors, agents, employees, or indemnities is against public policy and is void. Nothing in this section shall prohibit any person from purchasing insurance from an insurance company authorized to do business in the State of Ohio for his own protection or from purchasing a construction bond.

COMMENT:

A provision in a construction contract requiring that the promisor obtain liability insurance naming the promisee as an additional insured is not null and void due to the applications of RC § 2305.31 and is not contrary to public policy: *Brzeczek v. Standard Oil Co.*, 4 Oh. App. 3d 209 4 OBR 313.447 NE2d 760.

In a case where the promisor is an independent contractor of the promisee, RC § 2305.31 prohibits a provision in a construction contract in which the promisor agrees to indemnify the promisee for the promisee's own negligence. Such indemnity clause is void as against public policy: *Durgin v. Dugan & Meyers Construction, Inc.*, 7 Oh App. 3d 326, 7 OBR 423, 455 NE2d 694.

OREGON

30.140 Effect of indemnification provision in construction agreement.

(1) Any provision in a construction agreement which requires a person to indemnify another against liability for damage arising out of death or bodily injury to persons or damage to property caused or contributed to by the negligence of the indemnitee in the design or by the sole negligence of the indemnitee in the inspection of the work that is the subject of the construction agreement is enforceable only if the indemnitee secures or maintains insurance covering such risks for the protection of the indemnitor.

(2) In no event shall the indemnification obligation under such provisions be greater than the limits of the insurance secured by the indemnitee.

(3)   As used in this section, "construction agreement" means any written agreement for the construction, alteration, repair, improvement or maintenance of any building, highway, road excavation or other structure, project, development or improvement attached to real estate including moving, demolition or tunneling in connection therewith. No provision of this section shall be construed to apply to a "railroad" as deed in ORS 763.010. (1973 c.571 §§1.2)

COMMENT:

This statute disallows broad form and intermediate form indemnification clauses in construction contracts unless insurance covering the indemnitor's obligation is procurred by the indemnitee, and then only to the limits of insurance coverage.

Refers to *Sears, Roebuck and Company v. Montgomery Elevator Company,* No. A7902 00828; CA A23627; Court of Appeals of Oregon, 1983.

PENNSYLVANIA

§491. Preparation of plans; giving or failure to give directions; indemnification agreement.

Every covenant, agreement or understanding in, or in connection with any contract or agreement made and entered into by owners, contractors, subcontractors or suppliers whereby an architect, engineer, surveyor or his agents, servants or employees shall be indemnified or held harmless for damages, claims, losses or expenses including attorneys' fees arising out of: (1) the preparation or approval by an architect, engineer, surveyor or his agents, servants, employees or invitees of maps, drawings, opinions, reports, surveys, change orders, designs or specifications, or (2) the giving of or the failure to give directions or instructions by the architect, engineer, surveyor or his agents, servants or employees provided such giving or failure to give is the primary cause of the damage, claim, loss or expense, shall be void as against public policy and wholly unenforceable.

1970, July 9, P.L. 484, No. 164 § 1, effective in 60 days.

COMMENT:

This statute voids all hold harmless agreements where (a) the indemnitee is an architect, engineer or surveyor and (b) liability is due to a design error or error in supervision, where the supervision error is the primary cause of damage.

Refer to *Bush v. Chicago and Northwestern Transportation Corp.*, Civ. A. No. 79-907, U.S. District Court, E.D. Pennsylvania, 1981.

RHODE ISLAND

6-34-1. Construction indemnity agreements.

(a) A covenant, promise, agreement or understanding in, or in connection with or collateral to a contract or agreement relative to the design, planning, construction, alteration, repair or maintenance of a building, structure, highway, road, appurtenance, and appliance, including moving, demolition, and excavating connected therewith, pursuant to which contract or agreement the promisee, or its independent contractors, agents or employees has hired the promisor to perform work, purporting to indemnify the promisee, or its independent contractors, agents or employees or indemnitees against liability for damages arising out of bodily injury to persons or damage to property proximately caused by or resulting from the negligence of the promisee, its independent contractors, agents, employees, or indemnitees is against public policy and is void. Provided that this section shall not affect the validity of any insurance contract, workmen's compensation or agreement issued by an insurer.

(b) Nothing in this section shall prohibit any person from purchasing insurance for his own protection or from purchasing a construction bond.

COMMENT:

1. Prior Indemnity Agreements.
Arms length contractual agreements to indemnify entered into before enactment of this section are not against public policy and are thus enforceable. *Vaccaro v. E.W. Burman, Inc.* - R.I. -, 484 A.2d 880 (1984).

2. Agreements Prohibited.
This section, by its express terms, invalidates any agreement in which a party seeks indemnification from another for the consequences of its own or its agent's negligence: however, the legislature has not prohibited the use of all indemnification contracts in te construction industry. *Cosentino v. A.F. Lusi Constr. Co.,* - R.I. -, 485 A.2d 105 (198).

3. Agreements Permitted.
There is nothing in this section that bars a general contractor from attempting to secure indemnification from a subcontractor for claims resulting from negligence on the part of the subcontractor or of any subcontractor employed by the subcontractor. *Cosentino v. A.F. Lusi Constr. Co.,* -R.I. -, 485 A.2d 105 (1984).

SOUTH CAROLINA

§32-2-10. Hold harmless clauses in certain construction contracts void as against public policy.

Notwithstanding any other provision of law, a promise or agreement in connection with the design, planning, construction, alteration, repair or maintenance of a building, structure, highway, road, excavating, purporting to indemnify the promisee, its independent contractors, agents, employees, or indemnitees against liability for damages arising out of bodily injury or property damage proximately caused by or resulting from the sole negligence of the promisee, its independent contractors, agents, employees, or indemnitees is against public policy and unenforceable. Nothing whereby the promisor shall indemnify or hold harmless the promisee or the promisee's independent contractors, agents, employees or indemnitees against liability for damages resulting from the negligence, in whole or in part, of the promisor, its agents or employees. The provisions of this section shall not affect any insurance contract or workmen's compensation agreements; nor shall it apply to any electric utility, electric cooperative, common carriers by rail and their corporate affiliates or the South Carolina Public Service Authority.

History: 1980 Act No. 466, eff. June 9, 1980.

COMMENT:

This statute voids broad form hold harmless agreements in construction contracts which purport to indemnify the indemnitee for its sole negligence.

Refer to *McCain Manufacturing Corp. v. Rockwell International Corp.*, Cir. A. No. 80-1266-1, U.S. District Court D, South Carolina, Charleston Division, 1981.

SOUTH DAKOTA

56-3-7. Interpretation of contract of indemnity - Application of rules. In the interpretation of a contract of indemnity, the rules set forth in §§ 56-3-8 to 56-3-15, inclusive, are to be applied, unless a contrary intention appears.

56-3-8. Indemnity against liability - Recovery by person indemnified. Upon an indemnity against liabililty, expressly, or in other equivalent terms,unless a contrary intention appears, the person indemnified is entitled to recover upon becoming liable.

56-3-9. Indemnity against claims, demands or damages -Recovery by person indemnified, payment required. Upon an indemnity against claims or demands, or damages or costs expressly, or in equivalent terms, unless a contrary intention appears, the person indemnified is not entitled to recover without payment thereof.

56-3-10. Indemnity against claims, demands or liability - Matters embraced in contract. Unless a contrary intention appears, an indemnity against claims or demands, or liability, expressly, or in other equivalent terms, embrace the costs of defense against such claims, demands, or liability incurred in good faith, and in the exercise of reasonable discretion.

56-3-11. Defense by indemnitor of actions against indemnified-Right of person indemnified to conduct defense. Unless a contrary intention appears, the person indemnifying is bound, on request of the person indemnified, to defend actions or proceedings brought against the latter in respect to the matters embraced by the indemnity; but the person indemnified has the right to conduct such defenses, if he chooses to do so.

56-3-12. Neglect of person indemnifying to defend the person indemnified conclusive. If after request, the person indemnifying neglects to defend the person indemnified, unless a contrary intention appears, a recovery against the latter suffered by him in good faith, is conclusive in his favor against the former.

56-3-13. Notice of action or proceedings against indemnified not received by indemnitor - Indemnitor not allowed to control defense - Judgment against indemnitor presumptive evidence. If the person indemnifying, whether he is a principal or a surety in the agreement, has not reasonable notice of the action or proceeding against the person indemnified, or is not allowed to control its defense, judgment against the latter is only presumptive evidence against the former unless a contrary intention appears.

56-3-14. Application of stipulation as to conclusiveness of judgment against person indemnified upon indemnitor. A stipulation that the judgment against the person indemnified shall be conclusive upon the person indemnifying, is inapplicable, unless a contrary intention appears, if the person indemnified had a good defense upon the merits which, by want of ordinary care, he failed to establish in the action.

56-3-15. Reimbursement of indemnitor. Where one, at the request of another engages to answer in damages whether liquidated or unliquidated, for any violation of duty on the part of the latter, he is entitled to be reimbursed in the same manner as a surety for whatever he may pay.

56-3-16. Indemnification of architect or engineer for own errors prohibited in construction contract. Construction contracts, plans and specifications which contain indemnification provisions shall include the following provision:

The obligation of the contractor shall not extend to the liability of the architect or engineer, his agents or employees arising out of

(1) the preparation or approval of maps, drawings, opinions, reports, surveys, change orders, designs or specifications, or

(2) the giving of or the failure to give directions or instructions by the architect, or engineer, his agents or employees provided such giving or failure to give is the primary cause of the injury or damage.

56-3-17. Conflicting provision in construction contract unlawful and unenforceable. Any indemnification provision in construction contract in conflict with § 56-3-16 shall be unlawful and unenforceable.

56-3-18. Indemnity agreement void as to liability for negligence in a construction, repair or maintenance of structure or equipment. A covenant, promise, agreement or understanding in, or in connection with or collateral to, a contract or agreement relative to the construction, alteration, repair or maintenance of a building, structure, appurtenance and appliance, including moving, demolition and excavating connected therewith, purporting to indemnify the promisee against liability for damages arising out of bodily injury to persons or damage to property caused by or resulting from the sole negligence of the promisee, his agents or employees or indemnitee, is against the policy of the law and is void and unenforceable.

COMMENT:

Indemnification agreement was void as against public policy in the case where the only basis for indemnitee's liability to the injured party was indemnitee's sole negligence. *Chicago & North Western Transportation Co. v. V & R Sawmill, Inc.,* 501 F. Supp. 278 (1980).

TEXAS

Art. 249d. Construction contracts: indemnification of architects or engineers; covenants

Any covenant or promise in or in connection with or collateral to any contract or agreement made and entered into by any owner, contractor, subcontractor or supplier relative to the construction, alteration, repair or maintenance of a building, structure, appurtenance, road, highway, bridge, dam, levee, or other improvement to or on real property, including moving, demolition and excavating connected therewith, whereby a registered architect or registered engineer or his agents, servants, or employees is indemnified or held harmless by the contractor who is to perform the work from liability for bodily injury or death to persons or damage to property of any person or expenses in connection therewith caused by or resulting from defects in plans, designs or specifications prepared, approved or used by such architect or engineer or negligence of such architect or engineer in the rendition or conduct of professional duties called for or arising out of the contract or agreement and the plans, designs or specifications which are a part thereof shall be deemed void as against public policy and wholly unenforceable; provided, however, that this act shall not apply to a contract of insurance or workers' compensation agreement, nor to an owner of an interest in real property and persons employed solely by such owner, and this Act shall not prohibit nor render void or unenforceable any covenant or promise to indemnify or hold harmless such owner, and persons employed solely by such owner, or any covenant or promise to allocate, release, liquidate, limit, or exclude liability between the owner or other person for whose account a contract or agreement within the scope of this section is being performed on the one hand and a registered architect or registered engineer on the other hand, in connection with contracts and agreements of the class described above and further provided that this Act shall not apply to any contract or agreement whereby an architect or engineer or their agents, servants or employees is indemnified from liability for their negligent acts other than those described above or for the negligent acts of the contractor, any subcontractor, anyone directly or indirectly employed by any of them or anyone for whose acts any of them may be liable.

Amended by Acts 1981, 67th Leg., p. 2162, ch. 504 § 1, eff. Aug. 31, 1981.

COMMENT:

This statute allows only comparative fault indemnification of an architect, engineer, or surveyor where the liability arises out of the design or professional duties of the architect.

UTAH

13-8-1. Construction industry - Agreements to indemnify. - A covenant, promise, agreement or understanding in, or in connection with or collateral to, a contract or agreement relative to the construction, alteration, repair or maintenance of a building, structure, highway, appurtenance and appliance, including moving, demolition, and excavating connected therewith, purporting to indemnify the promisee against liability for damages arising out of bodily injury to persons or damage to property caused by or resulting from the sole negligence of the promisee, his agents or employees, or indemnitees is against public policy and is void and unenforceable.

64

This act will not be construed to affect or impair the obligations of contracts or agreements, which are in existence at the time it becomes effective.

COMMENT:

This statute voids broad form hold harmless clauses in construction contracts which purport to indemnify the indemnitee for his sole negligence.

For a discussion of this statute, refer to *Shell Oil Company v. Brinkerhoff - Signal Drilling Company*, No. 18084, Supreme Court of Utah, 1983.

VIRGINIA

§11-4-1. Certain indemnification provisions in construction contracts declared void. - Any provision contained in any contract relating to the construction, alteration, repair or maintenance of a building, structure or appurtenance thereto, including moving, demolition and excavating connected therewith, or any provision contained in any other contract relating to the construction of projects other than buildings by which the contractor performing such work purports to indemnify or hold harmless another party to the contract against liability for damage arising out of bodily injury to persons or damage to property suffered in the course of performance of the contract, caused by or resulting solely from the negligence of such other party or his agents or employees, is against public policy and is void and unenforceable.

This section shall not affect the validity of any insurance contract, workers' compensation agreement or other agreement issued by an admitted insurer.

The provisions of this section shall not apply to any provision of any contract entered into prior to July 1, 1973. (1973, c. 273; 1974, c. .30.)

COMMENT:

This statute voids broad form hold harmless clauses in construction contracts which attempt to shift liability for the indemnitee's sole negligence.

For a clarification of the case law relative to this statute, see *Richardson v. Econo-Travel Motor Hotel Corporation* Civ. A. No. 82-0280-A, U.S. District Court, E.D. Virginia, Alexandria Division, 1982.

WASHINGTON

4.24.115 Validity of agreement to indemnify against liability for negligence relative to construction, alteration, improvement, etc., of structure or improvement attached to real estate

A covenant, promise, agreement or understanding in, or in connection with or collateral to, a contract or agreement relative to the construction, alteration, repair, addition to, subtraction from, improvements to, or maintenance of, any building, highway, road, railroad, excavation or other structure, project, development, or improvement attached to real estate, including moving and demolition in connection therewith, purporting to indemnify against liability for damages arising out of bodily injury to persons or damage to property caused by or resulting from the sole negligence of the indemnitee, his agents or employees is against public policy and is void and unenforceable.

COMMENT:

Where a party is injured as a result of the concurrent negligence of both a contractor and the owner of the premises where an accident occurred, § 4.24.115, proscribing indemnification clauses shielding indemnitees from liability arising from their sole negligence, does not prevent the owner from recovering from the contract or on an indemnity agreement entered into between them. *Steinke v. Boeing Co.*, (D.C. Mont. 1981), 525 F. Supp. 234.

A guaranty of which is in essence a contract of indemnity, made for valuable consideration and as an inducement to the entering into and performing of a separate building-construction contract, is not subject to the provisions of § 4.24.115, which invalidates terms of construction contracts holding harmless one party for his own negligence, nor is such a guaranty an agreement involving a disclaimer of negligence or liability seeking to exonerate, in advance, the recipient for the consequences of his negligence or misconduct. *National Bank v. Equity Investors*, 81 Wash.2d 886, 506 P.2d 20 (1973).

WEST VIRGINIA

§ 55-8-14. Agreements to indemnify against sole negligence of the indemnitee, his agents or employees against public policy; no action maintainable thereon; exceptions.

A covenant, promise, agreement or understanding in or in connection with or collateral to a contract or agreement entered into on or after the effective date of this section [June 6, 1975] relative to the construction, alteration, repair, addition to, subtraction from, improvement to or maintenance of any building, highway, road, railroad, water, sewer, electrical or gas distribution system, excavation or other structure, project, development, or improvement attached to real estate, including moving and demolition in connection therewith, purporting to indemnify against liability for damages arising out of bodily injury to persons or damage to property caused by or resulting from the sole negligence of the indemnitee, his agents or employees is against public policy and is void and unenforceable and no action shall be maintained thereon.

This section does not apply to construction bonds or insurance contracts or agreements. (1975. c.117.).

COMMENT:

This statute disallows broad form hold harmless clauses in construction contracts which attempt to indemnify the indemnitee for its sole negligence.

WYOMING

§ 30-1-131. Provisions for indemnity in certain contracts; invalidity.

(a)   All agreements, covenants or promises contained in, collateral to or affecting any agreement pertaining to any well for oil, gas or water, or mine for any mineral, which purport to indemnify the indemnitee against loss or liability for damages for:

(i)   Death or bodily injury to persons;

(ii)   Injury to property; or

(iii) Any other loss, damage or expense arising under either (i) or (ii) from:

(A)   The sole or concurrent negligence of the indemnitee or the agents or employees of the indemnitee or any independent contractor who is directly responsible to such indemnitee; or

(B)   From any accident which occurs in operations carried on at the direction or under the supervision of the indemnitee or an employee or representative of the indemnitee or in accordance with methods and means specified by the indemnitee or employees or representatives of the indemnitee, are against public policy and are void and unenforceable to the extent that such contract of indemnity by its terms purports to relieve the indemnitee from loss or liability for his own negligence. This provision shall not affect the validity of any insurance contract or any benefit conferred by the Worker's Compensation Law (§g 27-12-101 to 27-12-805] of this state. (Laws 1969. ch. 46, § 1; 1977, ch. 145, §1.)

COMMENT:

The clear language of this section voids and makes unenforceable any agreement to the extent that it seeks to indemnify an indemnitee for his own negligence, regardless of the character of the negligence sought to be protected. See *Mountain Fuel Supply Co. v. Emerson*, 578 P.2d 1351 (Wyo. 1978).

CHAPTER III

IDENTIFICATION AND EVALUATION OF HOLD HARMLESS AGREEMENTS

The primary responsibility in any effort to properly manage the consequences of assumed liability is to identify the sources of such assumption. Unfortunately, the very nature of the environment in which the liability is created can involve almost any member of an organization—it could be the purchase of cleaning supplies by the janitor or a decision to acquire a subsidiary by the board of directors. For this reason, a constant awareness of all activities of the firm must be maintained by the person responsible for the identification of assumed liability.

As has been previously indicated, contracts take many forms. Oral contracts are often entered by the contracting parties and no record is ever made of the agreements. Fortunately, legal restrictions limit the validity of certain contracts to only those reduced to writing.

Even when contracts are written, one of the aspects of the hold harmless agreement which makes it a special problem for the risk manager and the insurance man is the difficulty of identifying and evaluating such a clause. Often, this type of agreement is one among many sections of a contract. Rarely are the clauses identified by any title. Such agreements vary, as has already been stressed, in language and scope with virtually no limit beyond the imagination of the drafters.

This chapter consists of various examples drawn from actual contracts. Each example, quoted precisely with only unnecessary identifying information omitted, is followed by a brief evaluation and related comments.

70

Each of the examples has been classified in relation to the degree of liability transferred by the contract. These classifications are defined as follows:

LIMITED FORM—This classification applies to agreements requiring indemnification for occurrences arising out of the indemnitor's operations.

INTERMEDIATE FORM—This classification applies to agreements requiring indemnification for all occurrences arising out of the indemnitor's operations, excluding only the liability of the indemnitee arising from his sole negligence.

BROAD FORM—This classification applies to agreements requiring complete indemnification of the indemnitee for all occurrences arising out of the indemnitor's operations without reference to negligence.

These examples are intended only to serve as a guide to assist in the identification of hold harmless agreements. The actual drafting of an agreement and the legal evaluation of any agreement should be only attempted by those whose competence has been proven in this particular legal arena.

EXAMPLES OF INDEMNITY AGREEMENTS

The examples illustrated here have been divided into seven broad categories. The categories are:

1. Construction Contracts

    (AIA Document 201, Broad Form Agreements, Intermediate Form Agreements, Limited Form Agreements)

71

2. Purchase Order Agreements

   (Broad Form Agreements, Intermediate Form Agreements)

3. Lease of Premises Agreements

   (Broad Form, Incidental Agreement, Waivers of Rights, Waiver of Subrogation)

4. Maritime Agreements

   (Bareboat Charter, Vessel Repair, Master Repair Contract—U.S. Navy)

5. Equipment Lease Agreements

   (Machine Tools, Automotive Equipment—Truck Line, Private Passenger Automobile, Electronic Data Processing)

6. Service Agreements

   (Agreement to provide bus service for college students)

7. Absolute Liability

   (Construction Agreement—Demolition Contract)

I. CONSTRUCTION AGREEMENTS

This section is devoted to a series of hold harmless clauses which have appeared in a variety of industry situations. As the reader will observe, most have interchangeable verbiage and a casual perusal will not be sufficient to accurately determine their dissimilarities. These examples are for informational purposes only and should not be used as recommendations for types of forms to be used.

The possible exception is the AIA Document, A201. This particular form may be recommended because its intent and the resulting consequences are relatively well known and understood.

CONSTRUCTION AGREEMENT—INTERMEDIATE FORM

The American Institute of Architects, General Conditions of the Contract for Construction, AIA Document A201.

INDEMNITY PROVISION:

4.18.1 The Contractor shall indemnify and hold harmless the Owner and the Architect and their agents and employes from and against all claims, damages, losses and expenses including attorneys' fees arising out of or resulting from the performance of the Work, provided that any such claim, damage, loss or expense (1) is attributable to bodily injury, sickness, disease or death, or to injury to or destruction of tangible property (other than the Work itself) including the loss of use resulting therefrom, and (2) is caused in whole or in part by any negligent act or omission of the Contractor, any Subcontractor, anyone directly or indirectly employed by any of them or anyone for whose acts any of them may be liable, regardless of whether or not it is caused in part by a party indemnified hereunder.

4.18.2 In any and all claims against the Owner or the Architect or any of their agents or employes by any employe of the Contractor, any Subcontractor, anyone directly or indirectly employed by any of them or anyone for whose acts any of them may be liable, the indemnification obligation under this Paragraph 4.18 shall not be limited in any way by any limitation on the amount or type of damages, compensation or benefits payable by or for the Contractor or any Subcontractor under workmen's compensation acts, disability benefit acts or other employe benefit acts.

4.18.3 The obligations of the Contractor under this Paragraph 4.18 shall not extend to the liability of the Architect, his agents or employes arising out of (1) the preparation or approval of maps, drawings, opinions, reports, surveys, Change Orders, designs or specifications, or (2) the giving of or the failure to give directions or instructions by the Architect, his agents or employes provided such giving or failure to give is the primary cause of the injury or damage.

COMMENT:

Much controversy and litigation have resulted from the difficulty of delineating lines of responsibility between the architect or engineer and the contractor. Increased construction activity, greater complexity of construction techniques, procedures and sequences and the growing complexity of the practices of architecture and engineering have led to an increase in the possibility of errors and the resulting accidents.

The architect's recent problems began with *Day vs. National U.S. Radiator Corp., 128 Sou.(2nd) 660, 1961.* This case involved the accidental death of a plumbing subcontractor's employe in an explosion which occurred when he tested a domestic hot water boiler prior to installation of a relief valve. His survivors, barred from tort liability recovery against the general contractor, sued the architect for failure to inspect the hot water system prior to its testing by the plumbing contractor. The architect was required by the contract to make periodic inspections, but the plumbing contractor had not notified him that the heater was being installed. Nevertheless, a Louisiana lower court held the architect negligent for improper inspection of job progress and rendered a judgment in excess of the architect's $50,000 professional liability limit. The appellate court not only upheld the decision, but increased the judgment substantially.

The Louisiana supreme court reversed the decision on the grounds that the architect had no duty to inspect. Nevertheless, precedent had been set for contractors' employes to look to the architect for remedy beyond that afforded by workers' compensation statutes. Needless to say, the Day case was a landmark decision. Practicing architects became increasingly concerned over their professional liability exposure.

The responsibility of the architect and his relationship to the owner and contractor are dependent upon the construction approach selected. The architect's services may terminate at completion of drawings and specifications; he may act as both designer and builder in rare instances; or, more commonly, the architect employs a mixture of the two approaches. He renders certain services during construction and exercises certain control. It is in this approach that it is most difficult to clearly delineate the duties and responsibilities of owner, contractor and architect.

The increased propensity of members of the public to bring claims against the architect for negligent acts has concerned the AIA in recent years. While a majority of claims were being settled or dropped before reaching the litigation stage, the architectural profession probably was becoming alarmed over cost and availability of adequate professional liabilty insurance.

These forces set the stage for inclusion of a standard indemnification clause in the revision of the AIA *General Conditions of the Contract of Construction* in 1966. For three years, AIA committees had been considering such a change and worked in liaison with committee of the Association of General Contractors. The final product was Article 4.18 of the General Conditions. The architects were primarily interested in avoiding involvement in third party claims arising from employes of contractors who were limited to workers' compensation benefits. The Day decision clearly demonstrated the architect would be consistently subjected to "shotgun" type suits from claimants who felt the workers'

75

compensation laws provided inadequate remedy for their injuries. AIA contends it was never its intent to transfer liability for professional mistakes to the contractor, but was attempting to avoid suits from the contractor's employes.

The new hold harmless had the apparent endorsement of both AIA and AGC committees. However, the reaction of state AGC chapters was loud and immediate. The AGC seized upon the new wording and interpreted it as an attempt to transfer to the contractor a significant portion of the architect's liability arising from accidents at the job site, even though Article 4.18.3 went on to state "The obligation under this paragraph shall not extend to any claim, damage, loss or expense which is attributable in whole or in *substantial* part to a defect in drawings or specifications prepared by the architect."

AGC people apparently felt this wording was ambiguous and would result in a greater degree of liability being assumed by the contractor. They felt this put member contractors in the position of assuming either "uninsurable" liabilities or incurring substantial additional insurance costs to protect themselves against claims resulting from the architect's negligence.

The fears of the contractors were shared by most of the major casualty insurers, who took a strong stand opposing the new AIA indemnification clause and stated or implied their unwillingness to insure the contract. The American Surety Association evaluated the agreement as imposing additional liabilities upon the contractor which might result in uninsured losses and impair or prevent completion of the job causing surety claims. This organization urged its member companies to encourage revision of the indemnity clause by making it difficult and costly to insure.

One large casualty group, which is also a major writer of architects professional liability insurance, recognized the severity of the indemnification clause but indicated a willingness to insure it for additional premium and for select clients.

The end result of this controversy was a new conference of AIA, AGC and casualty insurance representatives in an effort to agree on a standard indemnification clause which would be acceptable to architects and contractors and insurable at a reasonable cost. AIA felt its intentions were misunderstood. While concerned about increasing claims for professional negligence and the difficulty in clearly establishing the legal responsibilities of all parties, it was not the intent of AIA to transfer liability for professional mistakes to the contractor.

The revised indemnity clause broadened the liability which would be retained by the architect by providing that the contractor would not be liable for preparation or *approval* of maps, drawings, opinions, reports, surveys, change orders, designs or specifications, or the giving or *failure* to give instructions if it is the cause of injury. This language is more specific than the previous edition and the substitution of *primary* cause for *substantial* cause seems to reduce the probability of the contractor being held responsible for the architect's acts.

The very nature of the relationships between owner, architect and contractor is such that legal responsibilities of each party vary with the construction job to be performed—and this is as it should be. We will no doubt continue to have litigation involving the agency relationship between owner and architect, but the indemnification agreement should be as lucid and consistent as possible. This eleventh edition of AIA General Conditions seems to accomplish this objective for those construction jobs performed under this contract.

Note that 4.18.1(a) closely tracks the general liability policy definition of "bodily injury" and "property damage." Section 4.18.1(b) labels the contract as intermediate form since the contractor assumes liability for joint negligence of contractor-owner and/or architect.

Section 4.18.2 removes any possible limitation on benefits due to the operations of workers' compensation or similar law as being the maximum limit applicable to the liability assumed by the contractor as respects the owner and/or architect. This grew out of the Day case referred to previously.

Finally, note that 4.18.3 specifically limits the liability assumed by the contractor as respects the architect, to essentially non-professional acts of the architect. Freedom of the contractor from the responsibility of assuming this type of liabilty tracks rather closely with the exclusion in the contractual liability coverage normally afforded, and thus makes the contract basically insurable under the usual contractual coverage.

As pointed out in previous discussion, however, there is difference in that as respects supervision the contract relieves the contractor only if the architect's acts are the *primary* cause of the injury or damage while the usual contractual coverage does not include *primary* as a qualification in the exclusion of coverage.

Although AIA Document 201 was editorially revised in April 1970, the indemnity provisions were not altered. This seems to indicate again that proper cooperation between the various parties involved in a contractual relationship is the only means of achieving an equitable relationship.

CONSTRUCTION AGREEMENT—BROAD FORM

Indemnification of owners (not railroads)—excluding maritime operations.

INDEMNITY PROVISION:

Responsibility, Risk, Blame, etc. **The Contractor shall indemnify and save harmless the Owner from and against all losses, claims, demands, payments, suits, actions, recoveries and judgments of every nature and description brought or recoverable against it or them by reason of any act or omission of the Contractor, his agent or employes, in the execution of the work or in consequence of any negligence or carelessness in guarding the same.**

The Contractor shall assume all risk and bear any loss or injury to property or persons occasioned by neglect or accident during the progress of work until the same shall have been completed and accepted. He shall also assume all blame or loss by reason of neglect or violation of any state or federal law or municipal rule, regulation or order. The Contractor shall give to the proper authorities all required notices relating to the work, obtain all official permits and licenses and pay all proper fees. He shall make good any injury that may have occurred to any adjoining building, structure or utility in consequence of this work.

COMMENT:

Although the first paragraph of this clause is limited form, involving assumption only for act or omission of contractor, the second paragraph is broad form in that the contractor assumes all risk for any loss occasioned by neglect or accident by inference of *any party*.

Note that the assumption of liability by the contractor goes beyond the coverage afforded by standard forms of contractual liability coverage because they are limited by definition of "property damage" to injury to or destruction of *tangible* property. The possible loss or injury to the owner as a result of violation of any state or federal law could well be in form that is not "destruction of tangible property."

CONSTRUCTION AGREEMENT–BROAD FORM

Indemnification of owners (not railroads)–excluding maritime operations.

INDEMNITY PROVISION:

The Contractor shall indemnify and save harmless the Owners, the Architect, and their officers and employes, from all claims, loss, damage, injury, liability, costs and expenses of whatsoever kind or nature (including attorney's fees) howsoever the same may be caused resulting directly or indirectly from the nature of the work covered by the contract; and without limiting the generality of the foregoing, the same shall include injury or death to any person or persons and damage to any property, including that of the Owner.

COMMENT:

In this contract the contractor is indemnifying the owners and architects for injury or death to any person including the contractor's employes. Therefore, the contractor could be in the position of defending the owner from a suit for damages by the contractor's employe. In view of the limitations of benefits under the workers' compensation laws of most states, an attempt by an injured employe to seek additional benefits outside the workers' compensation laws is not unusual. This would be covered by the standard contractual liability form, assuming the owner is not a public authority.

There are other assumptions by the contractor which are not covered. Some of these are: (a) bodily injury or property damage arising out of professional services, since the indemnitees include the architect; (b) property damage to owner's property if contractor is exercising physical control over it; (c) damage or injury of "whatsoever kind or nature" may go beyond damage to *tangible property*, may be "expected" and may be due to loss of use of work completed

80

by the contractor, to collapse of completed work or to failure of work completed by contractor to serve the intended purpose, all outside the scope of coverage.

CONSTRUCTION AGREEMENT–BROAD FORM

Indemnification of owners used by major rubber goods manufacturer.

INDEMNITY PROVISION:

Contractor assumes entire responsibility and liability for losses, expenses, demands and claims in connection with or arising out of any injury, or alleged injury (including death) to any person, or damage, or alleged damage, to property of Owner or others sustained or alleged to have been sustained in connection with or to have arisen out of or resulting from the performance of the work by the Contractor, his subcontractors, agents, and employes, including losses, expenses or damages sustained by Owner, and agrees to indemnify and hold harmless Owner, his agents, and employes from any and all such losses, expenses, damages, demands and claims and agrees to defend any suit or action brought against them, or any of them, based on any such alleged injury or damage, and to pay all damages, cost and expenses in connection therewith or resulting therefrom.

COMMENT:

This agreement clearly includes a broader assumption of liability than is afforded cover under standard contractual liability provisions. The term "caused by accident" or "occurrence" found in the insuring agreements of the contractual form is not found in the assumption of liability. In other words, the contractor has assumed liability for loss or damage "resulting from the performance of the work by the contractor" without regard to the loss or damage being caused by accident.

CONSTRUCTION AGREEMENT—BROAD FORM

Agreement used by major aerospace company.

INDEMNITY PROVISION:

Contractor agrees that it will indemnify and hold harmless aerospace company and its respective officers, agents and employes from any loss, cost, damage, expense and liability by reason of property damage, personal injury, or both such damage and injury of whatsoever nature or kind arising out of or as a result of any negligent act or negligent failure to act in connection with the performance of the work by Contractor, its employes, agents and subcontractors, and Contractor agrees that the Public Liability and Property Damage Insurance (including Automobile Public Liability and Property Damage Insurance) which it is required to maintain pursuant to the article hereof entitled "Insurance" shall cover the obligations set forth above.

COMMENTS:

Personal injury is specifically indicated as being assumed by contractor as well as "damage and injury of whatsoever nature or kind." Although contractor is required to insure the obligations assumed, it may be that standard contractual liability cover would be held not to include much of the "whatsoever nature or kind" liability which has been assumed. Operational exposures should be carefully analyzed to make certain that such exposures are picked up by contractor's contractual liability cover.

CONSTRUCTION AGREEMENT—BROAD FORM

Agreement used by educational institution.

INDEMNITY PROVISION:

The Contractor shall hold harmless from and indemnify the Owner against all claims, suits, actions, costs, counsel fees, expenses, damages, judgments or decrees, by reason of any person or persons or property being damaged or injured by the Contractor or any of his subcontractors, or any person employed under said Contractor, or under any of his subcontractors, or in any capacity during the progress of the work, whether by negligence or otherwise.

COMMENT:

Since standard contractual liability forms provide coverage for legal liability based on negligence (negligence of the indemnitor, the indemnitee, or joint indemnitor/indemnitee) this clause goes beyond the grant of coverage and any "or otherwise" claims for injury or damage would probably not be covered.

CONSTRUCTION AGREEMENT—BROAD FORM

Agreement used by major oil company (not used as drilling agreement).

INDEMNITY PROVISION:

Contractor assumes and agrees to hold harmless, indemnify, protect, and defend Oil Company against any and all liability for injuries and damages to Contractor himself and to Contractor's employes, agents, subcontractors and guests, third parties or otherwise, incident to or resulting from any and all operations performed by Contractor under any of the terms of this contract.

COMMENT:

The phrases "any and all liability" and "incident to or resulting from any and all operations" serve to pick up substantially more liability than is covered under the terms and conditions of standard contractual liability insurance.

83

CONSTRUCTION AGREEMENT–BROAD FORM

Indemnification of railroads.

INDEMNITY PROVISION:

The Contractor shall be solely responsible for and shall indemnify and save harmless the Railway Company from and against all liability, loss, costs, detriments, damages and expense which the Railway Company may incur, sustain or be subjected to on account of the death of or injury to the Contractor and any subcontractors, and deaths of or injuries to any employes or agents of the Contractor or any subcontractors, caused by, arising out of or in any way connected with the work to be performed hereunder, or while the Contractor or any such subcontractors, employes or agents are on or near the site of the work or the premises of the Railway Company, without regard to whether any such deaths or injuries are caused by or attributable in whole or in part to the negligence of the Railway Company, its employes or agents, the condition of the premises, or otherwise, and notwithstanding any other provisions herein contained to the contrary.

COMMENT:

As the wording indicates, the agreement is Broad Form in scope, with the contractor agreeing to hold the railway company harmless for all liability arising out of the work "to be performed" or even while contractor is on or near the work site, regardless of whether the injury is the fault of the railroad or otherwise.

It is not possible to tell, of course, from the small portion of the agreement quoted above whether the party is exposed to the operation of railroad trains or not, which is a distinction as far as rating is concerned.

84

CONSTRUCTION AGREEMENT—BROAD FORM

Indemnification of owner (not railroads) excluding maritime operations.

INDEMNITY PROVISION:

1. The work provided for in this contract shall be done under the supervision of and subject to at all times to the inspection of the Chief Engineer of the Company (hereinafter called the "Engineer") or his duly authorized representative, and his decision as to the true construction and meaning of the contract and of the related plans, if any, shall be final and binding upon both parties. Any additional drawings or explanations necessary to detail and illustrate the work shall be furnished by the Engineer, and the parties agree to conform to and abide by the same. The Contractor shall provide sufficient safe and proper facilities at all times for inspection and general supervision of the work by the Company or the Engineer.

9. The Contractor agrees to rebuild, restore and repair or indemnify and hold the Company harmless against liability for any and all injuries and damages to the property of the Company, arising directly or indirectly from, or in any way referable to or occurring in connection with the work done hereunder, whether caused by the negligence of the Contractor, or employes, or otherwise.

10. The Contractor shall assume all responsibility for the work and shall indemnify and save harmless the Company against any and all claims for or relating to labor and materials furnished for or in connection with the work and against all claims for damages or profits to the use of any invention, patent or patent right in performing or contributing to the work.

11. The Contractor shall assume sole liability for injury to its employes and to any and all persons employed upon or in connection with the work hereby contemplated, whether by it or by any subcontractor, and for injury to employes of the Company or to the public with respect both to persons and property. The Con-

tractor shall indemnify and save harmless the Company with respect to all claims for or relating to all of such injuries or any of them.

COMMENT:

In this contract the contractor assumes liability for all injuries and damages even if caused by other than the contractor, despite the fact that the owner maintains close supervision.

Note that the contractor is assuming liability for damage to owner's property, which may be in contractor's care, custody or control and therefore not covered by usual insurance.

Note the assumption by contractor of responsibility for patent infringement, which is not covered by usual insurance.

In this agreement contractor assumes sole liability for injury to its employes, even if injured by agent of company or subcontractor and thus might have to defend suit by own employe against a third party.

CONSTRUCTION AGREEMENT—INTERMEDIATE FORM

Agreement used by electric utility firm.

INDEMNITY PROVISION:

The Contractor shall and does hereby agree to indemnify, save harmless and defend the Purchaser from the payment of any sum or sums of money to any person whomsoever on account of claims or suits growing out of injuries to persons, including death, or damage to property caused by the Contractor, his employes, agents or subcontractors or in any way attributable to the performance and prosecution of the work herein contracted for,

including (but without limiting the generality of the foregoing), all claims for service, labor performed, materials furnished, provisions and supplies, board of men, injuries to persons or damage to property, liens, garnishments, attachments, claims, suits, costs, attorneys' fees, costs of investigation and of defense. It is the intention of this paragraph to hold the Contractor responsible for the payment of any and all claims, suits, or liens, of any nature and character, in any way attributable to or asserted against the Purchaser, or the Purchaser and the Contractor, or which the Purchaser may be required to pay. In the event the liability of the Contractor shall arise by reason of the *sole negligence* of the Purchaser and/or the sole negligence of the Purchaser's agents, servants or employes, then and *only* then, the Contractor shall not be liable under the provisions of this paragraph.

COMMENT:

The claims assumed by the contractor under the terms of this clause go substantially beyond the insuring agreements of the standard contractual liability endorsement. What appears to be a concession on the part of the purchaser in the last sentence—relieving contractor of purchaser's sole negligence—is nothing more than a statement of purchaser's common law liability which would exist without such a statement.

CONSTRUCTION AGREEMENT—LIMITED FORM

Indemnification of owners (not railroad)—excluding maritime operations.

INDEMNITY PROVISION:

18.1 Contractor's Surface Equipment: Contractor shall assume liability at all times, regardless of whether the work is being performed on a footage basis or on a day work basis, for damage to or destruction of Contractor's surface equipment, including all drilling tools, machinery, and applicances for use above the surface, regardless of when or how such damage or destruction occurs, and Owner shall be under no liability to reimburse Contractor for any such loss except as to any loss or damage thereto occurring during the time that the operation of Contractor's equipment has been taken over by Owner as provided for in Par. 7 hereof.

18.2 Contractor's In-hole Equipment—Footage Basis: Contractor shall assume liability at all times while work is being performed on a footage basis for damage to or destruction of Contractor's in-hole equipment, including liability to reimburse Contractor for any such loss except as to any loss or damage thereto occurring during the time that the operation of Contractor's equipment has been taken over by Owner as provided for in Par. 7 hereof and except as provided for in Par. 13.2.

18.7 Underground Damage: Owner agrees to indemnify Contractor for any and all sums which Contractor shall become liable by final judgment to pay to any third party for damages resulting from operations under this contract on account of injury to, destruction of, or loss or impairment of any property right in or to oil, gas, or other mineral substance or water, if at the time of the act or omission causing such injury, destruction, loss, or impairment, said substance had not been reduced to physical possession above the surface of the earth, and for any loss or damage to any formation, strata, or reservoir beneath the surface of the earth.

18.9 Indemnity by Contractor: Contractor agrees to protect, indemnify, and save harmless the Owner from and against all claims, demands, and causes of action in favor of Contractor's employes or third parties on account of personal injuries or death or on account of property damages (other than property damages as hereinabove in this Par. 18 specifically provided for) arising out of the work to be performed by Contractor hereunder and resulting from the negligent acts or omissions of Contractor, Contractor's agents, employes, and subcontractors.

COMMENT:

This contract, which involves oil well drilling, is Limited Form since the contractor is holding the owner harmless only for negligent acts or omissions of the contractor, contractor's agents, employes and subcontractors (Section 18.9).

There are other contractual provisions which are of interest, however. Note that contractor is holding owner harmless for all damage to contractor's equipment, even if loss is caused by owner (Sections 18.1 and 18.2) except under special circumstances. This could have the effect of invalidating contractor's insurance on equipment since it is in effect a waiver of subrogation.

Note, too, that although owner is holding contractor harmless for underground damage, it is an indemnity of final judgment only and does not, apparently, include reimbursement of defense costs.

II. PURCHASE ORDER AGREEMENTS

This group of indemnity clauses seems to indicate that this type clause uniformly has the vendor or seller assuming the liability of the vendee or purchaser. There is illustrated one exception to this general position, but it is not uncommon to find situations in which the purchaser does, in fact, assume the liability or some liability of the seller in a purchase order transaction.

PURCHASE ORDER AGREEMENT–BROAD FORM

Excluding agreement involving construction work or erection or installation of the indemnitor's goods or products.

INDEMNITY PROVISIONS:

The Vendor agrees to indemnify and save harmless the Corporation and its agents, representatives, and employes from any and all charges, claims and causes of action by third persons, including, but not limited to agents, representatives and employes of the Vendor and of the Corporation, based upon or arising out of any damages, losses, expenses, charges, costs, injuries or illness sustained or incurred by such person or persons resulting from or in any way, directly or indirectly, connected with the performance or nonperformance of this Agreement, of the vending services provided for hereunder, or the performance of or failure to perform any work or other activity related to such vending services; provided, however, that notwithstanding the foregoing, the Vendor does not agree to indemnify and save harmless the Corporation, its agents, representatives and employes from any charges, claims or actions based upon or arising out of any damages, losses, claims, expenses, charges, costs, injuries or illness sustained or incurred as the sole result of the negligence of the Corporation, its agents, representatives or employes. In the event a claim is filed against the Corporation for which the Vendor is to be held liable under the terms of this agreement, the Corporation will promptly notify the Vendor of such claim and will not settle such claim without the prior written consent of the Vendor.

COMMENT:

This agreement is considered a Broad Form type because the vendor is assuming liability in the event of joint negligence of the vendor and corporation. The corporation retains liability only for its sole negligence.

Note that under this situation it would be possible for an employe of the vendor to sue the corporation for an on-the-job injury and to derive ultimate recovery from the vendor.

Coverage under the standard contractual liability language is not as broad as the assumption of liability by the vendor under this agreement. For example, the assumption of liability by the vendor includes damages which would fall under the "sistership" exclusion of the policy.

PURCHASE ORDER AGREEMENT—BROAD FORM

Excluding agreement involving construction work or erection or installation of the indemnitor's goods or products.

INDEMNITY PROVISION:

During the term of this agreement Seller shall indemnify, hold free and harmless, assume legal liability for and defend Purchaser, its agents, servants, employes, officers, and directors, from any and all costs and expenses, including but not limited to, attorneys' fees, reasonable investigative and discovery costs, court costs and all other sums which Purchaser, its agents, servants, employes, officers, and directors may pay or become obligated to pay on account of any, all and every demand or claim, or assertion of liability, or any claim or action founded thereon, arising or alleged to have arisen out of Seller's use of Purchaser's premises, or Seller's performance of this agreement, or the operation of Seller's business, or any act or omission of Seller, his agents, servants or employes, whether such claim or claims, action or actions be for damages, injury to person or property, including Purchaser's property, or death of any person, made by any person, group or organization, whether employed by Seller or Purchaser, or otherwise, or for breach of warranty by Seller either expressed or implied.

COMMENT:

In this agreement reference is made to act or omission of seller, but it is only one of many situations for which seller holds purchaser harmless. "Act or omission of seller" does not modify the assumption of liability for "any, all and every demand or claim" arising out of "seller's use of purchaser's premises" so that seller would appear to have assumed liability regardless of fault; hence, the agreement is Broad Form.

91

Note the contract includes reference to breach of warranty of seller which, by definition, is not within contractual liability coverage. This, instead, is products liability insurance.

PURCHASE ORDER AGREEMENT—BROAD FORM

Excluding agreements involving construction work or erection or installation of the indemnitor's goods or products.

INDEMNITY PROVISION:

In consideration of your permitting us or our servants, agents, employes and representatives from time to time to enter upon or to place or maintain equipment upon premises owned or controlled by you for the purpose of servicing our account, we agree to indemnify and hold you harmless from any claim or loss arising in any manner out of the presence or activity of the undersigned or any such equipment, when such persons or equipment are on your premises for the purpose of performing services, delivering or displaying goods, or otherwise transacting business or dealing with you in the interest or on behalf of the undersigned, and notwithstanding such accident or damage may have been caused in whole or in part by your negligence.

In this connection, upon prompt notice from you, we agree to defend at our expense, any claim made against you arising out of our presence or the presence of any of our employes or representatives or arising out of the presence of our equipment on your premises.

COMMENT:

This agreement is clearly Broad Form since the indemnification is for any claim or loss arising from the indemnitor's presence regardless of whose fault it is.

In this particular agreement the assumption of liability is even for the indemnitee's liability under workers' compensation laws. The agreement would also extend to defend the indemnitee in the event of a negligence suit brought against it by the indemnitor's employe.

It is possible that this agreement could be construed by the indemnitee to include several situations which would not be covered under standard contractual liability provisions particularly in the property damage area. For instance, there would be no coverage for property damage to property used by the indemnitor.

PURCHASE ORDER AGREEMENT–BROAD FORM

Purchase order used by firm selling material over which it has exclusive market control.

INDEMNITY PROVISION:

9. Purchaser will assume that material supplied by seller is adequate and appropriate for purchaser's use and purchaser, in it's use of this material, will protect and save seller harmless in the event of any and all loss and any and all damage which may occur to seller through error or misuse of such material either within or outside the normal scope of the purchaser's business.

COMMENT:

In this agreement the parties to the typical purchase order agreement are reversed in that the purchaser is assuming the liability of the seller. The example is obviously broad form because the assumption of liability is neither defined nor restricted in any manner. It vividly illustrates the bargaining positions of the parties because the purchaser must have an absolute need if he is willing to contractually assume this degree of responsibility.

PURCHASE ORDER AGREEMENT – BROAD FORM

Purchase order used by major retail food chain.

93

INDEMNITY PROVISION:

Processor hereby agrees to indemnify and save harmless (indemnitee) from and against any and all losses, liabilities, costs, expenses, libels, suits, actions, claims and other obligations and proceedings whatsoever, including, without limitation, all judgments rendered against, and fines or penalties imposed upon, (indemnitee) and any reasonable attorney's fees and other expenses, incurred in connection therewith, which, directly or indirectly, may be payable, caused by, attributable to, arise by virtue of, or result from actual or alleged, (i) consumption or use of any food or grocery product sold or distributed to or through indemnitee (ii) breach of any guaranty, specification or warranty, express or implied, as to the quality or kind of any such product, including any contained in §1 above or related to raw materials, manufacture, production, processing, packaging, packing, sealing, storage or delivery, (iii) misbranding or other labeling deficiency of any such product, including inaccuracy or inadequacy of any specification, warning or other information on the label or other packaging thereof, or (iv) act or omission by Processor or any supplier, agent or employe of Processor other than indemnitee.

COMMENT:

This is an example of the current efforts on the part of retail food distributors to attempt to transfer to their suppliers liability for goods furnished to them for resale. This particular contract exhibits an unusual approach because the particular type liability exposure contemplated by the indemnitee is specified.

PURCHASE ORDER AGREEMENT—INTERMEDIATE FORM

Purchase order used by major oil refiner.

INDEMNITY PROVISION:

Contractor agrees to indemnify and save oil company, its co-owners, joint ventures, agents, employes and insurance carriers

94

harmless from any and all losses, claims, actions, costs, expenses, judgments, subrogations, or other damages resulting from injury to any person (including injury resulting in death), or damage (including loss or destruction) to property of whatsoever nature of any person arising out of or incident to the performance of the terms of this contract by Contractor (including, but not limited to, Contractor's employes, agents, subcontractors, and others designated by Contractor to perform work or services in, about, or attendant to, the work and services under the terms of this contract). Contractor shall not be held responsible for any losses, expenses, claims, subrogations, actions, costs, judgments, or other damages, directly, solely, and proximately caused by the negligence of oil company. Insurance covering this indemnity agreement shall be provided by Contractor.

COMMENT:

An unusual feature of this clause is the inclusion of the oil company's insurance carriers as parties indemnified by the contractor. Assuming that the contractor passes this assumed liability on to its insurance carrier through contractual liability coverage, this results in one insurance carrier indemnifying another insurance carrier, perhaps for liability properly recoverable under the second insurer's policy.

PURCHASE ORDER AGREEMENT—LIMITED FORM

Excluding agreements involving construction work or erection or installation of the indemnitor's goods or products, excluding assumption of liability for negligence of the indemnitee.

INDEMNITY PROVISION:

The Seller does further agree to indemnify and hold each of said Buyers harmless from and of any and all actions, suits or proceedings brought by any federal or state authorities against any one or more of said Buyers and/or any such beverage, health or beauty

95

aids, food, drug, device or cosmetic for the adulteration and/or misbranding and/or alleged adulteration or misbranding of any such beverage, health or beauty aids, food, drug, device or cosmetic within the meaning of any of said laws, state or federal and/or from and of all actions, suits or proceedings brought or commenced by any person against Buyers for the recovery of damages for the injury, illness and/or death of any person caused or alleged to have been caused by the consumption or use by such person of any beverage, food, drug, device or cosmetic, including any judgment rendered against Buyers in any such action, suit or proceeding and all fines, costs and expenses (including reasonable attorneys' fees) incurred by any one or more of said Buyers in connection with or as a result of any such action, suit or proceeding, provided that Seller received reasonable notice of the service of process upon any one or more of said Buyers in such action, suit or proceeding; provided further, that this indemnification shall not cover any claim for which Buyers may be legally responsible.

COMMENT:

This agreement represents a specific assumption of liability by the seller of liability it would ordinarily have in any event. It does pass on to the seller the costs of any action against the buyer.

It is noteworthy that the standard product liability provisions would not include payment of damages for adulteration or misbranding which would involve (a) loss or damage to the product itself and (b) the "sistership" exclusion. Consequently the liability assumed by the seller is not entirely covered by the insurance contract.

III. LEASE OF PREMISES AGREEMENTS

Although this type of agreement is most often seen, its form and consequence vary radically. The examples contained herein illustrate only a small group of the variations contained in lease of premises agreements.

It should be noted that many, if not all, lease of premises agreements hold the lessee responsible for liability arising out of the use of the premises and for damage to certain portions of the property under lease. These provisions must be treated before the lease is executed to avoid possible severe consequences. A special effort is usually required to locate these provisions because they may be located in different sections of the agreement and may not be titled as such in the agreement.

LEASE OF PREMISES AGREEMENT—BROAD FORM

Premises lease by shopping center.

INDEMNITY PROVISION:

Lessee shall indemnify and save harmless Lessor from and against any and all loss, cost (including attorneys' fees), damages, expense and liability (including statutory liability and liability under workmen's compensation laws) in connection with claims for damages as a result of injury or death of any person or property damage to any property sustained by . . .Lessee . . .all other persons . . .which arise from or in any manner grow out of any act or neglect on or about the Shopping Center by Lessee, Lessee's partners, agents, employes, customers, invitees, contractors and subcontractors.

COMMENT:

Note that statutory liability as well as common law liability is assumed by lessee. There may be certain statutory liability imposed on the lessor which has, by the terms of this clause, been passed on to lessee. Additionally, some jurisdictions do not permit the transfer of sole negligence in a lease agreement by deeming such transfer as contrary to public policy.

LEASE OF PREMISES AGREEMENT–"STANDARD FORM"

Commercial property lease.

INDEMNITY PROVISION:

(3) Premises shall be used for _____ purposes and no other. Premises shall not be used for any illegal purposes; nor in violation of any valid regulation of any governmental body, nor in any manner to create any nuisance or trespass; nor in any manner vitiate the insurance or increase the rate of insurance on premises.

(5) Lessee shall repair partitions, all glass and plate glass, elevators, electric and plumbing fixtures, and all machinery whatever in leased premises. Lessee shall be liable for and shall hold Lessor harmless in respect of: damage or injury to Lessor, premises, and property or persons of Lessor's other tenants, or anyone else, if due to act or neglect of Lessee, or anyone in his control or employ. Lessee shall at once report in writing to Lessor any defective condition known to him which Lessor is required to repair, and failure to do so shall make Lessee responsible for damages resulting from such defective condition.

(23) At termination of this lease, Lessee shall surrender premises and keys thereof to Lessor in same condition as at commencement of term, natural wear and tear only excepted.

COMMENT:

The above provisions are taken from a more or less standard lease of premises agreement which is an *incidental written agreement* under the standard liability insurance provisions. Even though this is the case, there are certain assumptions of liability which are not covered under the usual liability contract.

The illustrated provisions are some of the features which may present problems:

Item 3 governs use of premises. Note it is a violation of the lease to use property in any manner which vitiates insurance or increases the rate of insurance on the property. In this particular lease, "insurance" is undefined and presumably could be any form of property coverage.

Item 5 states that lessee is liable for damage to lessor's property if due to "act or neglect" of lessee. This would fall under the care, custody or control exclusion of the liability contract, and would require fire legal liability coverage.

Item 23 is included because it makes no exception other than natural wear and tear in condition of premises upon surrender to lessor, which would apparently give no relief in the event premises were damaged by fire.

LEASE OF PREMISES AGREEMENT–INCIDENTAL AGREEMENT

Commercial property lease.

INDEMNITY PROVISION:

The Lessee agrees to indemnify and save harmless the Lessor against and from any and all claims by or on behalf of any person or persons, firm or firms, corporation or corporations, arising from the conduct of or management about the demised premises, or from any accident in or on the demised premises, and will further indemnify and save the Lessor harmless against and from any and all claims arising from any breach or default on the part of the Lessee in the performance of any covenant or agreement on the part of the Lessee to be performed pursuant to the terms of this lease, or arising from any act or negligence of the Lessee, or any of its agents, contractors, servants, employes or licensees, and from and against all costs, counsel fees, expenses and liabilities incurred in or about any such claim or action proceeding brought thereon; and in case any action or proceeding be brought against the Lessor by reason of any such claim, the Lessee upon notice from the Lessor covenants to resist or defend at Lessee's expense such action or proceeding by counsel reasonably satisfactory to the Lessor.

COMMENT:

This is an *incidental written agreement* ordinarily considered to be covered under the standard provisions for general liability insurance.

Note, however, that the lessee agrees to save the lessor harmless from all claims arising from a breach in the lease. A question could arise as to whether a breach or default could give rise to an accident resulting in bodily injury or property damage "neither expected nor intended from the standpoint of the insured" which is in the policy definition of "occurrence."

Another point is that the lessee covenants to defend lessor using counsel reasonably satisfactory to the lessor. The decision as to whether or not to defend, and the selection of counsel are rights reserved to the insurance company under standard provisions and hence the lessee could not rely on his insurance to make good this contractual obligation.

LEASE OF PREMISES AGREEMENT–"WAIVER OF RIGHTS"

Commercial property.

INDEMNITY PROVISION:

Lessee, as a material part of the consideration to be rendered to the Lessor hereby, waives all claims against Lessor for damages to the goods, wares and merchandise in, upon or about said premises and for injuries to Lessee, his agents or invitees in or about said premises, and Lessee will hold Lessor exempt and harmless from any damage and injury to any such person or to the goods, wares and merchandise of any such person, arising from the use of the premises by Lessee or from failure of Lessee to keep the premises in good condition and repair as herein provided.

COMMENT:

In this agreement the lessee has not assumed any liability but has in effect waived a right of action against the lessor. This could have the effect of invalidating the lessee's property insurance contract under certain conditions.

LEASE OF PREMISES—COMMON LAW LIABILITY FOR ACCIDENTAL DAMAGE TO PROPERTY OF LESSOR OR LESSEE

Waiver of subrogation.

CONTRACTUAL PROVISION:

To the extent that it is lawful to do so,

(1) Lessor hereby expressly waives and releases any cause of action or right of recovery which Lessor may have hereafter against the Lessee for any loss or damage to the leased premises, or to the contents thereof belonging to either, caused by fire, explosion or any other risk covered by insurance and,

(2) Lessor shall obtain a waiver from any insurance carrier with which Lessor carries fire, explosion or any other risk coverage insuring the building and other improvements releasing its subrogation rights against leasee.

101

COMMENT:

Under this provision found in a lease agreement, the common law liability that the tenant may have to the lessor is abrogated. The specific reference is to insurance for the purpose of avoiding rights which may be subrogated to the lessor's insurer.

Generally the insurance carrier for the lessor would pay for losses to the owner of the leased building and proceed against the tenant if his negligence caused the damage. The insurer acquires this right of action under the subrogation clause in the insurance contract.

In this situation, the lessor is required to secure from his insurer, if insurance is carried, a waiver of this right of subrogation. Although practice varies, there normally is a charge by the insurer for giving up this right under the insurance contract.

It is obvious the lessee has achieved a preferred status in this portion of the lease. If equity is to be shared by the parties, the waivers should be established for both lessee and lessor.

Alternate solutions to the problem include:

(1) The lessor and lessee may have their respective interests shown on each of their respective insurance policies. They would have the insurance contracts indicate the other party as an additional insured, "as his interest may appear."

(2) Each party could purchase fire and certain other legal liability insurance coverage. This would provide indemnity for their negligently causing fire damage to the other party's property.

(3) Each party could attempt to have the care, custody

or control exclusions deleted from their respective general liability contracts. Despite the difficulty normally encountered in this approach, it is this particular exclusion that creates the problem.

While these comments may only be "related" to risk assumption contractually, the situation is so prevalent that the subject should receive proper notice. It is not intended that the liability involved in these situations be treated as contractual liability otherwise described.

IV. MARITIME AGREEMENTS

As is typical with most considerations, maritime indemnity agreements have unique characteristics. Maritime agreements are unusually varied in form and content. It is most important that their analysis be left to one who is especially well informed in the general scope of the maritime industry.

MARITIME AGREEMENT–BAREBOAT CHARTER

INDEMNITY PROVISION:

II. The Vessel shall be delivered to the Charterer at the port of _____, and being on her delivery tight, staunch, strong, and well and sufficiently tackled, appareled, furnished, and equipped, and in every respect seaworthy and in good running order, condition and repair so far as the exercise of due diligence can make her. The delivery to the Charterer of said vessel and the acceptance of said vessel by the Charterer shall constitute a full performance by the Owner of all the Owner's obligation hereunder, and thereafter the Charterer shall not be entitled to make or assert any claim against the Owner on account of any representations or warranties expressed or implied, with respect to said vessel. Owner's responsibility for repairs or renewals occasioned by latent defects in the vessel, her machinery or appurtenances, existing at the time of delivery under the Charter, and not discoverable on survey, shall be limited solely to the reasonable cost of such repairs or renewals.

V. Charterer shall man, victual, fuel, maintain, navigate and supply the vessel at its sole cost and expense and shall pay all charges and expenses of every kind and nature whatsoever incident thereto, and pay all fines and penalties levied against the vessel, it being understood that Owner retains no dominion, control, possession or command of said vessel during the term of this Charter.

VI. Charterer shall at no time misuse or abuse the vessel and shall handle it carefully at all times. Charterer shall comply with all applicable federal, state, municipal and local laws of the U.S.A. or any other country having jurisdiction over the vessel and with the rules, orders, regulations, directives and requirements of any departments, commissions and bureaus having authority over the vessel, and with all local ordinances and regulations, and shall indemnify and hold Owner harmless from all libels, maritime liens, claims, seizures, charges, encumbrances, suit, or penalties which may be imposed upon or filed against Owner or upon the vessel by federal, state, municipal and local laws of the U.S.A. or any other country having jurisdiction over the vessel and with the rules, orders, regulations, directives and requirements of any departments, commissions and bureaus having authority over the vessel, and with all local ordinances and regulations, and shall indemnify and hold Owner harmless from all libels, maritime liens, claims, seizures, charges, encumbrances, suit, or penalties which may be imposed upon or filed against Owner or upon the vessel by federal, state, municipal, or local authority of the U.S.A. or any other country having jurisdiction over the vessel, or by any departments, commissions, or bureaus thereof by reason of any asserted violation by Charterer of such laws, rules, orders, ordinances, regulations, directives or requirements.

COMMENT:

The above provisions are from a contract concerning the charter of a vessel by the owner to the charterer, which requires a particular form of insurance. It would appear that paragraphs II and V, taken together, clearly place the responsibility for *protection and indemnity* losses on the charterer, and that paragraph VI clearly makes charterer responsible for an action *in rem* against the vessel.

MARITIME AGREEMENT–BROAD FORM

Vessel repair contract used by major oil bulk carrier.

INDEMNITY PROVISION:

The Contractor shall take proper safeguards for the prevention of accidents or injury to person or property. Contractor shall indemnify and hold harmless the Owner and Charterer, their agents, the vessel and its crew from all claims, suits, actions, in personam or in rem, and all loss and expense, including reasonable attorneys' fees, on account of injuries to, death of, and damage to the property of any person whomsoever, including the parties hereto, their agents and employes, as well as any third person, arising from, growing out of, or caused directly or indirectly by any operation incident to the performance of the work undertaken by the Contractor or any of its subcontractors during the duration of this agreement, even though caused or contributed to by a negligent act or omission of the Owner and Charterer, their agents or employes, or by unseaworthiness of the vessel. Neither final inspection, discharge of the vessel from Contractor's custody, or final payment shall relieve the Contractor of responsibility for faulty materials or workmanship, and unless otherwise specified it shall remedy any defects due thereto and bear the loss for any damage to person or property resulting therefrom in accordance with all terms and conditions contained in the within paragraph.

COMMENT:

This clause sweeps in product warranty (and product liability) as well as a broad assumption of liability on the part of the contractor. Note that the wording requires the contractor to indemnify the owner for damages to the owner's property even though such loss could be caused by the owner's negligence.

105

MARITIME AGREEMENT—LIMITED FORM

Master repair contract for repairs and alteration of vessels used by U. S. Navy.

INDEMNITY PROVISION:

The Contractor indemnifies and holds harmless the Government, its agencies and instrumentalities, the vessel and its owners, against all suits, actions, claims, costs or demands (including, without limitation, suits, actions, claims, costs or demands resulting from death, personal injury and property damage) to which the Government, its agencies and instrumentalities, the vessel or its owner may be subject or put by reason of damage or injury (including death) to the property or person of any one other than the Government, its agencies, instrumentalities and personnel, the vessel or its owner, arising or resulting in whole or in part from the fault, negligence, wrongful act or wrongful omission of the Contractor or any subcontractor, its or their servants, agents, or employes.

COMMENT:

There appears to be a possibility that a party not a party to the contract between the U. S. Navy and the contractor may be a beneficiary under the terms of this clause. The Government, the vessel or its owner are to be indemnified and held harmless and it is assumed that the repair and alteration contract would be between only the Government (U.S. Navy) and the contractor.

V. EQUIPMENT LEASE AGREEMENTS

Leasing equipment has become a major factor in the typical commercial activity and the trend seems to be accelerating. With this growth, a companion growth has developed in contracts purporting to facilitate the leasing function.

The agreements now associated with leasing are as varied as the type of equipment being leased. It now appears that most means of communication, transportation and production are or will be subject to the terms of a lease agreement.

The current evidence available seems to indicate that the more sophisticated the object being leased, the significantly more severe the indemnity provisions of the lease. It is most important that these leases be evaluated carefully because the parties to the basic negotiations of the typical lease document are not oriented toward the difficulties which may arise out of the lease as a result of the imposition of a severe hold harmless agreement.

EQUIPMENT LEASE AGREEMENT—MACHINE TOOLS

Equipment lease agreement.

INDEMNITY PROVISION:

The Lessee covenants that it will in respect of the Equipment

(a) **Pay the rentals promptly when due.**
(b) **Assume responsibility for them, as current values, against fire and loss or damage from whatever cause arising.**
(c) **Employ them only on work carried out on the Lessee's premises.**
(d) **Permit the Lessor to inspect them at all reasonable times.**
(e) **On termination of this agreement return them to the Lessor at the expense and risk of the Lessee.**

COMMENT:

The above is a paragraph from an equipment lease concerning a machine tool to be used on the premises of the lessee in its manufacturing operation.

While there is no specific assumption of liability for damage or injury to property of others in this particular lease (as a matter of fact, the question of liability for the faulty operation of the machine is not mentioned at all), it is interesting to note that the lessee makes an "all risk" assumption of responsibility for damage to the machine itself, regardless of negligence. This is, of course, not covered in a liability contract as the care, custody or control exclusion would prevail.

EQUIPMENT LEASE AGREEMENT—AUTOMOTIVE EQUIPMENT

INDEMNITY PROVISION:

4. Before settlement for the equipment rental, all known expenses of operation, including but not limited to rate errors necessitating charge backs, cost of labor connected with the loading or unloading of the vehicle, and all expenses of a like or similar character growing out of the operation of the equipment, shall be deducted from the equipment earnings, and if any such charges or amounts due the Lessee, a cash bond in the sum of $150 shall be required from the Lessor which bond shall be paid by deducting from the equipment earnings the sum of $10 each week from the beginning of the lease until the amount of the bond has been deposited. This bond shall be held by the company for a minimum period of 90 days after the cancellation or expiration of the lease. However, the release of the bond as herein provided shall in no way relieve the Lessor of his liability to the Lessee for any amounts which may thereafter be determined to be due to the Lessee as a result of such charge backs or other expenses.

108

5. The Lessee shall provide cargo insurance as required by law: However, the Lessor shall be responsible to the Lessee for the first $150 of such cargo loss or damage from whatever cause. In case of collision or upset, Lessor agrees to protect the cargo from any further damage, loss or theft and shall be responsible for any subsequent shortage, loss, damage or injury to such cargo.

8. Lessee shall maintain Public Liability and Property Damage Insurance as well as Workmen's Compensation Insurance and agrees to hold Lessor harmless from any such claim while said equipment is in the actual service of the Lessee; however, Lessor shall maintain at his own expense Public Liability and Property Damage Insurance which shall be effective while the equipment is parked, deadheading, bobtailing or otherwise being operated in any manner other than under pursuant to specific dispatch instructions from the Lessee; and the Lessor will save Lessee harmless from any loss, claim or liability while the equipment, or either unit thereof, is so used or employed. This shall be construed to mean that the Lessee will not be responsible for Public Liability, Property Damage, Workmen's Compensation or Cargo Insurance when the equipment is being used other than in connection with the transportation of freight under the authority and with the authorization of the Lessee, or when the same is being used in any manner except under and pursuant to dispatch instructions of the Lessee.

COMMENT:

The above clauses are from an equipment lease pertaining to the rental of automotive equipment by a truck line. This type of contract could be insured under the contractual liability coverage part of the general liability contract as there is no applicable automobile exclusion.

The lease provisions stipulate (Section 5) that lessor will pay for the first $150 of damage to cargo and will protect cargo from further damage. Since these assumptions pertain to property over which the lessor is exercising physical control they would be beyond the scope of standard contractual liability insurance coverage.

EQUIPMENT LEASE AGREEMENT–PRIVATE PASSEN-GER AUTOMOBILE

INDEMNITY PROVISION:

Lessee agrees to indemnify and hold Lessor free and harmless from any liability, loss, cost, damage or expense, including attorney's fees, which Lessor may suffer or incur as a result of any claims which may be made by any person, including but not limited to Lessee, its agents and employes, that arise out of or result from the manufacture, delivery, actual or alleged ownership, performance, use, operation, possession, selection, leasing and/or return of the vehicle, whether such claims are based on negligence, whether of Lessor or another, breach of contract, breach of warranty, absolute liability or otherwise.

COMMENT:

This condition of a lease for a private passenger automobile goes far beyond the normal scope of indemnification. This type agreement poses a difficult problem for two basic reasons: (1) most lessees do not recognize the obligations of the agreement; (2) the obligations are beyond the function of contractual liability insurance, since it makes reference to areas of liability which are not contemplated in contractual liability insurance forms.

EQUIPMENT LEASE AGREEMENT–DATA PROCESSING EQUIPMENT

INDEMNITY PROVISIONS:

Lessee shall and does hereby agree to indemnify and save Lessor harmless from any and all liability arising out of the ownership, selection, processing, leasing, renting, operation, control, use, maintenance, delivery and return of the equipment, but shall be credited with any amounts received by the Lessor with respect thereto from liability insurance procured by the Lessee.

COMMENT:

This agreement forms a part of a lease-purchase agreement for electronic data processing equipment. It obviously has the intent of passing on to the lessee-purchaser the entire responsibility of the existence, care and use of the equipment for the term of the agreement on the same basis as if the lessee-purchaser were the owner.

VI. SERVICE AGREEMENTS

As is true with leasing equipment, purchasing personal services is a current major development within the economy. The typical agreement is usually either very carefully constructed or only a conversation between the contracting parties.

In either event, the liability assumption is usually passed on to the party agreeing to perform the service. The unusual aspect of this type agreement is a common effort to define both quantitatively and qualitatively the risk being assumed. This effort is most difficult and extreme care must be exhibited during the negotiation stage to avoid major problems.

CONTRACT FOR SERVICES AGREEMENT

Agreement to provide bus transportation for college students within a college campus.

INDEMNITY PROVISION:

The contractor shall be responsible from the time of the beginning of operations, for all injury or damage of any kind resulting from

111

said operations, to persons or property regardless of who may be the owner of the property. In addition to the liability imposed upon the Contractor on account of personal injury (including death) or property damage suffered through the Contractor's negligence, which liability is not impaired or otherwise affected hereunder, the Contractor assumes the obligation to save the Owner harmless and to indemnify the Owner from every expense, liability or payment arising out of or through injury (including death) to any person or persons or damage to property (regardless of who may be the owner of the property) of any place in which work is located, arising out of or suffered through any act or omission of the Contractor or any Subcontractor, or anyone directly or indirectly employed by or under the supervision of any of them in the prosecution of the operations included in this contract.

COMMENT:

This agreement has two definitions of liability assumptions. The first relates to the "sole negligence" for "all injury or damage of any kind resulting from said operations." The second definition involves a description of the work area and the inclusion of this area as subject for transfer of liability. Other than the design of program aspects of the service being rendered, the agreement is a definition of common law.

CONTRACT FOR SERVICES AGREEMENT

Agreement to provide testing services for a new device developed by a major public utility firm.

INDEMNITY PROVISIONS:

LIABILITY—All persons furnished by you shall be considered your employes or agents and you shall be responsible for payment of all unemployment, social security and other payroll taxes, including contributions from them when required by law.

You agree to indemnify and save us and our customers harmless from any claims or demands (including the costs, expenses and reasonable attorney's fees on account thereof) that may be made: (1) by anyone for injuries to persons or damage to property including theft resulting from your acts or omissions or those persons furnished by you; or, (2) by persons furnished by you or your subcontractor under Workmen's Compensation or similar acts. You agree to defend us and our customers, at our request, against any such claim or demands against us or our customers for which you are responsible hereunder.

COMMENT:

This clause includes an effort to define the obligations of the parties to the extent that the contractor is specifically described as an independent contractor. This attempt does not appear to achieve the desired result because such efforts, for the most part, have been abrogated by court decisions based upon the circumstances of the damage and injury.

Otherwise, the clause is unique because it specifically includes theft as a condition. This no doubt is relative to the contract because the contractor was performing the service on the premises of the owner in the area of research and development activities.

It is also important to note the parties who become indemnities under the agreement. Not only the owner but also his customers are included for indemnification. The clause also demands defense for both the owner and his customers.

VII. ABSOLUTE LIABILITY

This situation involves the demolition of a building by implosion. Since this risk included not only those hazards normally attendant to demolition, but also the possibility of causing either closing down or impairing of a major interstate artery through the municipality, the agreements were designed with care by the parties to the contract.

The municipality required the following agreement which includes the owner general contractor, and the implosion subcontractor to jointly and severally become indemntors.

The undersigned owner, general contractor and subcontractor (hereinafter collectively referred to as "Indemnitors"), for and in consideration of the undertaking of the municipality to provide regular police, fire and other assistance during the Activity, and for other good and valuable consideration, the receipt and sufficiency whereof is hereby acknowledged by Indemnitors, do hereby jointly and severally covenant, undertake and agree that they, and each of them, will indemnify and hold harmless (without limit as to amount) the municipality and its officials, officers, employes and servants in their official capacity (hereinafter collective referred to as "Indemnitees"), and any of them, from and against all loss, all risk of loss and all damage (including expense) sustained or incurred because of or by reason of any and all claims, demands, suits, actions, judgments and executions for damages of any and every kind and by whomever and whenever made or obtained, allegedly caused by, arising out of or relating in any manner to the Activity, and to protect and defend Indemnitees, and any of them, with respect thereto.

The foregoing obligation by the Indemnitors shall be covered by appropriate insurance naming Indemnitees as additional named insured with aggregate limits of not less than $20,000,000. _____

purchased by Indemnitors from an insurance company duly

licensed to engage in the business of issuing such insurance in the State, such insurance to be evidenced by a certificate of binder which so provides and is delivered to the municipality prior to the issuance of any demolition permit for the Activity.

Indemnitors do not intend the obligation they undertake as expressed in this Instrument to insure to the benefit of any person or legal entity not named herein as Indemnitees. Indemnitors further agree and understand that a material part of the inducement to the municipality to provide the services which are part of the consideration for the obligation expressed in this Instrument are the representations made by Indemnitors, individually, or through their agents, about the nature of the Activity, including but not limited to the recitals in this Instrument and those appearing in or attached to the official minutes of the _____ _____ meeting with the Building Code Advisory Board of the municipality.

In an effort by the general contractor to indemnify the owner for his obligation to the municipality, the following agreement was executed.

Indemnification. General Contractor warrants that it is an independent contractor and agrees to indemnify and save harmless the Owner from and against any loss or expense by reason of any liability imposed by law upon the Owner and from and against claims against Owner for damages because of bodily injuries, including death, at any time resulting therefrom, accidents sustained by any person or persons on account of damage to property rising out of or in consequence of the performance of this Agreement, whether such injuries to persons or damage to property are due or claimed to be due to any negligence of general contractor, the Owner, their agents, servants, or employes or of any other person.

In an effort by the demolition subcontractor to indemnify both the owner and the general contractor for their liability the following agreement was executed.

Indemnification. Subcontractor warrants that it is an independent contractor and agrees to indemnify and save harmless the Owner, and general contractor, from and against any loss or expense by

115

reason of any liability imposed by law upon the Owner and general contractor and from and against claims against Owner and general contractor, for damages because of bodily injuries, including death, at any time resulting therefrom, accidents sustained by any person or persons on account of damage to property rising out of or in consequence of the performance of the Agreement, whether such injuries to persons or damage to property are due or claimed to be due to any negligence of General Contractor, the Owner, their agents, servants, or employes or of any other person.

It was only after these contracts were executed and the arrangements made with the authorities did the question of the legality of hold harmless agreements designed to transfer absolute liability come to the attention of the parties. Since it was determined that an effort to make such a transfer was at least questionable, it not illegal, the entire project was delayed several months while the question was debated. Unfortunately, the debate hinged most specifically on, "Why would this create any problem if we have valid insurance."

It is obvious that the liability insurance involved would not respond for assumed liability, if the assumption of such liability is illegal. This example reflects the unsuccessful attempt to use the hold harmless agreement to solve a complex legal situation which only created a more complicated legal entanglement.

CHAPTER IV

THE CONTROL OF LIABILITY CREATED BY HOLD HARMLESS AGREEMENTS

The sampling of hold harmless agreements in the previous chapter should indicate the importance of the subject of this chapter. Someone—the risk manager, an employe with insight into the depth of the problem and sufficient authority to deal with it or the firm's insurance adviser—must be responsible for the *control* of the possible liability created by the very existence of the scores—hundreds perhaps—of contracts into which a business or organization enters in a single week.

There is no intent that this chapter be mistaken for a discussion of the principles of risk management as such, but, the authors hold to the strong belief that the application of those principles to this particular problem is the best approach. Those principles and these suggestions can be adapted without difficulty to very nearly any size organization. It may be either a large corporation with its own risk management department entering into numerous contracts daily or, the subject may be a small business which will rely upon its lawyer and insurance men to establish the needed control.

ADMINISTRATIVE CONTROL PROGRAM

Regardless of the size of the organization, it is important that there be an orderly administrative program for control of hold harmless liability. This program depends upon policy, of course, but its proper working requires carefully thought out internal procedures.

The responsible person—risk manager, insurance manager, buyer or other official—needs to cultivate an understanding with everyone in his company who is involved with

117

contracts. That includes those who draw up the contracts offered by his company as well as those who accept contracts offered by others. All of these should be encouraged to stay in close touch with the risk manager, checking with his department regularly and informing him without fail of all contracts entered into.

Initially, the objective should be to give all such personnel a clear understanding of the grave risk hidden in the most innocuous-appearing contract and the need to submit such documents to the risk manager for evaluation. Experience has taught that many a capable business man whose acquaintance with the principles of risk and insurance is a passing one, if it exists at all, completely misses the point of a hold harmless clause. He needs to have it explained—perhaps several times—that the courts will not permit two parties to contract away the rights of third parties; that acceptance of a hold harmless clause in favor of someone else automatically transfers the obligations of the favored party to the accepting party; and that this species of contractual liability is both easy to overlook and vicious in its potentialities. In short, since the person responsible for risk management is seldom the person who commits his organization contractually, he must indoctrinate those who do make such commitments to acquire the habit of checking with him regularly and faithfully.

It is apparent in situations such as those described in Chapter III involving the waiver of subrogation in a lease agreement, the most advantageous involvement for the person responsible for control is during the contract drafting. As was true in that instance, once the contract has been communicated favorable alternatives are more difficult to identify.

In practically every organization a large number of the contracts entered into will be more or less routine. The control system can be ordered to this situation early in the game. To illustrate, some weeks or months of careful scrutiny will probably indicate that purchase orders from certain concerns, service contracts with certain concerns and various other more or less common contracts will have one or the other classification of indemnity agreement, if any. Once risk management has discerned this pattern, appropriate decisions can be made about dealing with the liability involved and the matter left to periodic auditing of such contracts.

The more dangerous area, obviously, is that of contracts which cannot be classified as "routine." With these, the proper indoctrination of all responsible personnel is of manifest importance. And, the essential point of that indoctrination is that the *risk manager must be brought into the picture early and without fail.* Again, it cannot be stressed enough that indemnity agreements are not easy to spot, are less easy to evaluate and can be inordinately hazardous. The risk manager or other official with responsibility for that function must be given an opportunity to perform these difficult tasks early enough to suggest a sound course.

The most imaginative and thorough administrative program of contractual liability control needs periodic review. It is quite possible, for instance, that some of its procedures are unnecessarily cumbersome—or not careful enough. Similarly, the cost of administering the system must be known and watched. *Control*—which depends upon knowledge of the facts—is the key objective. If the system is achieving this, fine; if not, it must be made to work.

BASIC CONTROL DECISIONS

On the basis of this identification and evaluation of the hazards inherent in the hold harmless provisions of the contractual flow, the person responsible for risk management must make his decisions about the treatment of these hazards. Or, he must present his recommendations to management for decision.

If this responsible party can properly establish his relative position, he may well be able to review all contracts prior to their being finally executed. When this position can be maintained, a basic opportunity exists which involves a recommendation to management to avoid entering the contract. Obviously, the consequences of assumed liability would have to be so severe as to make the contract otherwise unattractive, yet it is not uncommon for a department head to be so preoccupied with the benefit of the contract to his department that he not be sensitive to a provision as remote as "paragraph XXVII, Indemnity." Too often this apparently insignificant topic can adversely affect the financial stability of the entire organization.

If avoidance is inappropriate, as it most often must be, the considerations are generally as follows:

1. To what extent can the assumption of risk be reduced?

2. What risks can the organization afford to assume?

3. To what extent should the risk be transferred by means of insurance?

4. Can specific provisions of contracts be deleted, particularly those which involve risks which can be neither assumed nor transferred?

5. Broadly, what arrangements are possible in connection with the insurance coverage of the contractual hazard?

6. Is it possible to negotiate clearer contract language—especially to clarify and spell out a meeting of the minds of the parties on all points which seem likely to present future problems?

The matter of identifying and evaluating the hazards of assumed liability was covered in the previous chapter. However, it seems appropriate to note here that the control system and consideration of the points listed above and discussed below demands thoroughness and accuracy in identification and evaluation. Special exposures such as aircraft, watercraft, blasting, malpractice, etc., need to be watched for. Unique hazards are especially important. For instance, the organization with which the firm is contracting may be in the chemical or petroleum industry, or in atomic energy. Assumptions involving these can be particularly hazardous. Similarly, the relative size and strength of the contracting parties is important. Perhaps the contract in question calls for the firm to pick up the whole burden of the liability of a much larger concern. Of course, the control decisions must take into consideration the not always clear matter of public policy and the effects of a possible violation of this concept.

Reduction of Risk Assumed

The consideration of reducing the assumption the risk is both a general and a specific matter. Specifically, both parties to a contract may find it necessary to consider cutting the scope of the hold harmless clause to that which can be effectively and economically handled by insurance. The contract drafters—both sides—should be given a clear picture of the importance of the insurance function, not to speak of both its adequacies and shortcomings in contractual liability coverage. Further, one cannot overlook the element of uncertainty of court interpretation of this form of coverage and of the hold harmless agreement itself.

As a general matter, risk managers and others might do well to encourage less ready use of hold harmless clauses. As has been pointed out by numerous observers in recent years, the multiplication of these impositions has not only complicated business relationships but has raised costs as well. Wherever the unnecessary use of such a clause can be discouraged, the effect is in the direction of reduction in the amount of risk which must be assumed or otherwise provided for.

Self Assumption of Risk

Returning to the principal concern of the risk manager in dealing with a controlling assumed risk, it may well be that a given agreement or group of agreements present a risk which the corporation is willing simply to assume, without seeking insurance. Obviously, such cases will usually involve only minor and remote hazards, free of any element of catastrophe exposure. Assumption is out of the question if the loss, even though a remote contingency, could be large enough to wreck the corporate structure.

Extent of Transfer To Insurance

For such hazards as are to be covered by insurance, the risk manager must be absolutely certain of the coverage that he can obtain for his firm. He must also take into account the insurance protection, if any, of the other party. This is where the services of good agents or brokers are most important. There are not only the questions of arranging needed coverage, but also of the ability to obtain interpretations for the insurer when necessary, and the defense obligations involved.

Alteration of Contract Assumption Language

The best combination of reduction, self-assumption and insurance may leave some contractual assumptions unprovided for. At this point, it is felt, management must decide whether it will enter into such a contract at all. An alternative is to seek amelioration of the hold harmless language. Examples of such possible situations might include assumptions which extend to liability for acts of God, contingencies for which no insurance can be obtained, sole negligence, prohibitive coverage costs and the like. Short of simply staying out of the contractual relationship altogether, the only other choice seems to be to attempt to have the indemnity agreement softened or eliminated. This might not be as difficult as one thinks. Much depends upon the bargaining weight of the parties, as pointed out in the first chapter, but it does seem quite possible that the circumstances might sometimes dictate softening such an agreement.

Insurance Application

Chapter V goes into the details of contractual liability insurance. However, a few observations are in order here, since the scope of available coverage is an important consideration in establishing and maintaining control.

Many organizations today will be carrying blanket contractual liability insurance (though, as noted in the next chapter, the extent of such coverage varies and needs to be understood precisely in terms of the policy in use). Similarly, many businesses now carry umbrella liability insurance. Also, it may be that the liability insurance contracts of the risk have been modified through softening or deletion of various exclusions, a practice which has been followed to some extent by insurers in particular cases.

The authors suggest that consideration be given to obtaining blanket contractual liability insurance, on as broad a basis as possible. Various features of contractual liability coverage which can sometimes be negotiated include:

1. Have coverage made applicable to oral as well as written contracts.

2. Eliminate the word "accident" from the definition of "occurrence."

3. Include personal injury.

4. Employe coverage.

It might also be desirable to request that the contractual liability exclusion be removed from the insured's automobile policies. Also, it has sometimes been suggested that exclusions of explosion, collapse, underground hazards, malpractice, liquor liability and care, custody or control be eliminated if possible.

A prime consideration, of course, is that all coverage be written at *adequate limits.*

Costs are obviously never unimportant in decisions concerning control. The following will need study:

1. Contractual liability insurance premiums.

2. The effect of insured claims on experience rating and the insured's position with its insurer.

3. The effect of uninsured claims within deductible amounts, exclusions or exhausted limits.

4. In cost-plus contracts, the consequences of retrospective adjustments should be spelled out for both parties' policies.

5. Contractual coverage costs might be programed on an annual rather than an individual contract basis.

Clarity of Contract Language

Wherever possible—and it may well be possible more often than is at first supposed—the contract language should be revised for clarity. Definitions are very important—and often omitted. Some other points on which agreements should be clear include:

1. Responsibility for physical loss or damage to property of indemnitee, indemnitor, closely associated parties, and all other parties.

2. Business interruption, loss of income, expense resulting from physical loss of each of the above parties.

3. Responsibility for injury to persons, agents, or employes of the indemnitee, indemnitor, of closely associated parties, or to the public.

4. Spell out administrative problems and responsibility for costs related thereto.

5. Anticipate and make provisions for changes in nature of work over life of contract. Example: Occupancy of building before completion.

CONCLUSION

The central function must necessarily be one that includes an awareness of all the contractual obligations being considered: recommendations to management as to the consequences of obligations to be assumed; advices or suggestions on methods of reducing the risk to be assumed; reducing the resulting conditions which may tend to create or increase the chance of a loss; and taking the necessary steps to minimize the effect of the loss if it in fact does occur.

These are recognized as the ingredients of the classical method of handling risks. The proper application of these techniques are tantamount to the proper control function.

CHAPTER V

CONTRACTUAL LIABILITY INSURANCE IN THE 1/73 EDITION OF THE COMPREHENSIVE GENERAL LIABILITY INSURANCE PROGRAM[1]

Indemnification for liability assumed contractually is available through normal insurance techniques. Generally, the basic liability insurance contracts specifically exclude such liability with certain specific exceptions. These exceptions are defined as "incidental agreements" and basically represent ordinary situations which occur most commonly and, for the most part, are well defined over a long period of judicial precedent.

Beyond these basic exceptions, a separate and independent approach must be employed. This is the provision of a specific coverage part for liability assumed under contracts not defined as incidental contracts.

INCIDENTAL AGREEMENTS

The exceptions to this general statement are those contracts which are described as *Incidental Contracts* in the standard liability provisions. Coverage is provided under the basic policy for those so described. They are as follows:
1. A lease of premises.
2. An easement agreement, except in connection with construction or demolition operations on or adjacent to a railroad.
3. An undertaking to indemnify a municipality required by municipal ordinance, except in connection with work for the municipality.

1. This chapter treats contractual liability as found in the January, 1973 edition of the comprehensive general liability policy. Since it will be some time before the newer "occurrence" and "claims-made" forms of the commercial general liability program have completely replaced its use, this information continues to be relevant.

The following chapter, chapter VI, is devoted to the treatment of contractual liability in ISO's commercial general liability policies.

4. A sidetrack agreement.
5. An elevator maintenance agreement.

These "incidental contracts" are automatically covered under the basic liability policies without charge, and are subject to the same limits of liability, conditions, limitations and exclusions provided in the policy form. The coverage applies to bodily injury or property damage as defined in the policy and caused by an occurrence which takes place during the policy period within the policy territory.

Lease of Premises

Lease of premises takes in all portions of a real estate lease including incidental construction work to be done by the tenant. It is important to remember that this coverage does not apply to leases for personal property such as machinery and various industrial equipment or other types of personal property.

Some hold harmless contracts hold the lessee responsible for damage to property, both real and personal, leased to him or in his care, custody or control. Since the basic liability coverages are subject to the care, custody or control exclusion, there is no coverage for this portion of the contract unless the exclusion is deleted or the exposure handled in a manner described in Chapter III under Lease of Premises relating to waiver of subrogation.

Premises leased to parties who use the premises for selling, serving or giving of any alcoholic beverage have unique restrictions on the coverage available under these basic contract provisions. In situations where liability is imposed on owners or lessors by statute, ordinance or regulation, coverage is excluded for liquor liability.

A vessel chartered under a bareboat charter would not be considered "premises" under the definition in the policy and thus, there is no coverage for this exposure.

Easement Agreements

Easement agreements are covered except in connection with construction or demolition operations on or adjacent to a railroad. Railroad Protective Liability coverage is necessary to cover construction or demolition on, along, or adjacent to a railroad right of way.

Municipal Ordinances

Undertakings to indemnify a municipality required by municipal ordinance, except in connection with work for the municipality, are covered by basic liability insurance. It is important to note the *necessity* that the indemnification or hold harmless agreement be "required by ordinance." When work is being done *for* the municipality, specific coverage must be procured.

Sidetrack Agreements

Sidetrack agreements are covered automatically without specific premium charge. This is true whether the contract is undertaken directly with a railroad or with a sublessor.

Elevator Maintenance Agreements

An elevator maintenance agreement is covered without specific premium charge. The definition of elevator is very broad and means "any hoisting or lowering device to connect floors or landings, whether or not in service and all appliances thereof including any car, platform, shaft, hoistway, stairway, runway, power equipment and machinery; but does not include an automobile servicing hoist, or a hoist without a platform outside a building if without mechanical power or if not attached to building walls, or a hod or material hoist used in alteration, construction or demolition operations, or an inclined conveyor used exclusively for carrying property or a dumbwaiter used exclusively for carrying property and having a compartment height not exceeding four feet." Note that this definition is broad enough to apply to an escalator and, thus, to an escalator maintenance agreement.

Basic Policy Limitations

It is important to note the exclusions of standard liability insurance provisions relating to "incidental contracts." The care, custody or control exclusion was discussed under lease agreements. Unless this exclusion is deleted, specific coverage is necessary to provide protection for the bailment situation.

The collapse, explosion, and underground property damage exclusions are not applicable to incidental contracts.

Contracts covered must be written. Verbal contracts must be separately insured.

Leases or easements of waterfront property, including use of watercraft, appear to be covered including operation of the watercraft. The watercraft exclusion in regard to watercraft away from the premises of the named insured does not apply to an incidental contract.

War damage is excluded specifically from coverage for incidental and other insured contracts.

The liquor liability exclusion appears to apply to incidental contracts because of the reference to "the insured or his indemnitee." Although not specifically mentioned, an indemnitee is a beneficiary under a hold harmless agreement and a lessor leasing to a liquor distributor should check the tenant's policy to make sure that the proper coverage is provided in accordance with the applicable statute, ordinance or regulation. The exclusion would have to be removed to provide the proper coverage.

129

Another exclusion refers to any obligation for which the insured or any carrier as his insurer may be held liable under any workers' compensation or disability benefits law, or under any similar law.

There is no coverage under these agreements for the personal injury hazards of libel, slander, invasion of privacy, false arrest, or for patent infringement.

CONTRACTUAL LIABILITY COVERAGE

The indemnification for liability assumed under contracts which are not within the group described as "incidental contracts" must be specifically handled. This is accomplished through the provision of contractual liability insurance.

The basic liability coverages are extended through the addition of the contractual liability *coverage part* to the basic liability forms. This coverage part is a relatively self contained contract with the exception of certain "conditions" and "provisions" found in the basic form, since it includes a coverage clause, definitions, exclusions, and limits of liability.

Coverages   —   **Contractual Bodily Injury Liability**
                   Contractual Property Damage Liability

The contractual liability insuring agreement reads as follows:

The company will pay on behalf of the **insured** all sums which the **insured**, by reason of **contractual liability** assumed by him under any written contract of the type designated in the schedule for this insurance, shall become legally obligated to pay as damages because of

bodily injury or
property damage

130

to which this insurance applies, caused by an **occurrence**, and the company shall have the right and duty to defend and **suit** against the **insured** seeking damages on account of such **bodily injury** or **property damage**, even if any of the allegations of the suit are groundless, false or fraudulent, and may make such investigation and settlement of any claim or **suit** as it deems expedient, but the company shall not be obligated to pay any claim or judgment or to defend any **suit** after the applicable limit of the company's liability has been exhausted by payment of judgments or settlements.

Although this coverage provision seems self evident as to intent, the insurance form further refines this provision by specific definition of certain terms contained in the clause. One must fully comprehend these definitions before making any effort to interpret the coverage provided; moreover, since this insuring agreement becomes a part of the basic liability contract, the definitions contained in the basic contract also become an integral part of the study of coverage provided.

DEFINITIONS OF CONTRACTUAL LIABILITY COVERAGE TERMINOLOGY

The first group of definitions relate directly to the coverage clause of contractual liability insurance. These definitions are listed below in the order in which they appear.

1. INSURED

Named Insured means the person or organization named in the declarations of this policy.

Each of the following is an **insured** under this insurance to the extent set forth below:

(a)   if the **named insured** is designated in the declarations as an individual, the person so designated and his spouse;

(b) if the **named insured** is designated in the declarations as a partnership or joint venture, the partnership or joint venture so designated and any partner or member thereof but only with respect to his liability as such;

(c) if the **named insured** designated in the declarations as other than an individual, partnership or joint venture, the organization so designated and any executive officer, director or stockholder thereof while acting within the scope of his duties as such.

This insurance does not apply to bodily injury or property damage arising out of the conduct of any partnership or joint venture of which the insured is a partner or member and which is not designated in this policy as a named insured.

2.   CONTRACTUAL LIABILITY

"**Contractual Liability**" means liability expressly assumed under a written contract or agreement; provided, however, that **contractual liability** shall not be construed as including liability under a warranty of the fitness or quality of the **named insured's products** or a warranty that work performed by or on behalf of the **named insured** will be done in a workmanlike manner.

There have been recent developments in the contractual relationships in the construction contracts which have made this definition most significant. Many hold harmless agreements being used in the owner-contractor relationship have been extended to include such terminology as "to protect," "to defend" in addition to the usual "indemnify," "hold harmless," and "save harmless," provisions.

It seems apparent that this definition of contractual liability would include such an additional obligation, it would appear that the indemnitor's insurer would have both the duty and the right to "defend" the indemnitee.

The major problem arises out of an agreement in which no specific mention of "defense" is made. In the absence of "defense" in the agreement, there does not appear to be a definitive position as to the obligation of the indemnitor's insurer to defend the indemnitee.

The practical application of the consequences of such a moot question can give rise to involved legal entanglements when response is expected from the insurer. It is *not* recommended that the question be resolved *after* a claim has developed. To avoid this possible difficulty, it is suggested that the insurer expand this definition to specifically include "defense" of the indemnitee by endorsement to the contractual liability coverage part.

3. **BODILY INJURY**

Bodily Injury means bodily injury, sickness, disease sustained by any person which occurs during the policy period, including death at any time resulting therefrom.

4. **PROPERTY DAMAGE**

Property Damage means:

(1) physical injury to or destruction of tangible property which occurs during the policy period, including the loss of use thereof at any time resulting therefrom, or

(2) loss of use of tangible property which has not been physically injured or destroyed provided such loss of use is caused by an **occurrence** during the policy period.

5. **OCCURRENCE**

Occurrence means an accident, including continuous or repeated exposure to conditions, which result in **bodily injury** or **property damage** neither expected nor intended from the standpoint of the **insured**.

For the purpose of determining the limit of the company's liability, all **bodily injury** and **property damage** arising out of continuous or repeated exposure to substantially the same general condition shall be considered as arising out of one **occurance.**

6. SUIT

Suit includes any arbitration proceeding to which the **insured** is required to submit or to which the **insured** has submitted with the company's consent.

7. ARBITRATION

The company shall be entitled to exercise all of the insured's rights in the choice of arbitrators and in the conduct of any arbitration proceedings.

CONTRACTUAL LIABILITY EXCLUSIONS

The coverage provided by the contractual liability policy excludes or does not apply to the situations described in this section. Each individual contractual form should be evaluated because there is a lack of uniformity in this area.

1. To liability assumed by the insured under any **incidental contract**. This exclusion shifts coverage for **incidental contracts,** as defined, back to the basic general liability form.

2. (a) If the **insured** is an architect, engineer or surveyor, to **bodily injury** or **property damage** arising out of professional services performed by such insured, including

   (i) the preparation or approval of maps, drawings, opinions, reports, surveys, change orders, designs or specifications, and

   (ii) supervisory, inspection or engineering services;

   (b) If the indemnitee of the insured is an architect, engineer or surveyor, to the liability of the indemnitee, his agent or employes, arising out of

(i) the preparation or approval of maps, drawings, opinions, reports, surveys, change orders, designs, or specifications, or

(ii) the giving of or the failure to give directions or instructions by the indemnitee, his agents or employes, provided such giving or failure to give is the primary cause of the bodily injury or property damage.

This exclusion is the consequence of the efforts of a variety of interested parties, including contractors, architects, owners, and lawyers. It has been constantly refined and this latest edition, January 1, 1973, appears to have established a proper relationship between the contracting parties as it relates to these particular circumstances. Although some of the parties to contracts may not believe this exclusion serves their respective best interest, it does serve as a specific definition of coverage provided under insurance contracts.

3. To **bodily injury** or **property damage** due to war, whether or not declared, civil war, insurrection, rebellion or revolution or to any act or condition incident to any of the foregoing;

4. To **bodily injury** or **property damage** for which the indemnitee may be held liable

(a) as a person or organization engaged in the business of manufacturing, distributing, selling or serving alcoholic beverages, or

(b) if not so engaged, as an owner or lessor of premises used for such purposes,

if such liability is imposed

(i) by, or because of the violation of any statute, ordinance or regulation pertaining to the sale, gift, distribution or use of any alcoholic beverage, or

(ii) by reason of the selling, serving or giving of any alcoholic beverage to a minor or to a person under the influence of alcohol or which causes or contributes to the intoxication of any person;

but part (ii) of this exclusion does not apply with respect to liability of the indemnitee as an owner or lessor described in (b) above.

Insured should be made aware of this exclusion especially in states which have stringent dram shop laws, because a hold harmless agreement in a lease agreement or other contract might pass this liability on to the insured by contract.

5. To any obligation for which the **insured** or any carrier as his insurer may be held liable under any workmen's compensation, unemployment compensation or disability benefits law, or under any similar law.

This applies only to workers' compensation liability imposed by workers' compensation statutes directly upon the insured and does not appear to apply to compensation of another party assumed under contract.

6. To any obligation for which the **insured** may be held liable in an action on a contract by a third party beneficiary for **bodily injury** or **property damage** arising out of a project for a public authority; but this exclusion does not apply to an action by the public authority or any other person or organization engaged in the project.

Note that the exclusion applies only if the claim arises out of a project for a public authority but not to an action by the public authority or any other person or organization engaged in the project.

7. To **property damage** to

(a) property owned or occupied by or rented to the **insured,**

(b)   property used by the **insured**, or

(c)   property in the care, custody or control of the insured or as to which the **insured** is for any purpose exercising physical control.

This care, custody or control exclusion was previously discussed under "incidental contracts" and bailee's coverage should be sought to cover property of others in the care, custody or control of the insured.

8.   To **property damage** to premises alienated by the **named insured** arising out of such premises or any part thereof.

9.   To loss of use of tangible property which has not been physically injured or destroyed resulting from

(a)   a delay in or lack of performance by or on behalf of the **named insured** of any contract or agreement, or

(b)   the failure of the named **insured's products** or work performed by or on behalf of the **named insured** to meet the level of performance, quality, fitness or durability warranted or represented by the named insured;

but this exclusion does not apply to loss of use of other tangible property resulting from the sudden and accidental physical injury to or destruction of the **named insured's products** or work performed by or on behalf of the **named insured** after such products or work have been put to use by any person or organization other than an insured.

This is commonly called the "business risk" exclusion and attempts to carry out the intent in the products area of a general liability insurance that coverage is not afforded for what might be termed purely "business risk." Coverage is excluded when a product or work fails to perform the function or serve the purpose warranted or represented by the named insured.

10. To **property damage** to the **named insured's products** arising out of such products or any part of such products.

11. To **property damage** to work performed by or on behalf of the **named insured** arising out of the work or any portion thereof, or out of materials, parts or equipment furnished in connection therewith.

12. To damages claimed for the withdrawal, inspection, repair, replacement, or loss of use of the **named insured's products** or work completed by or for the **named insured** or of any property of which such products are withdrawn from the market or from use because of any known or suspected defect or deficiency therein.

Products recall or sistership liability coverage is sometimes available separately to pick up various expenses of withdrawing known or suspected defective products.

13. To **bodily injury** or **property damage** arising out of the ownership, maintenance, operation, use, loading or unloading of any **mobile equipment** while being used in any prearranged or organized racing, speed or demolition contest or in any stunting activity or in practice or preparation for any such contest or activity;

14. To **bodily injury** or **property damage** arising out of the discharge, dispersal, release or escape of smoke, vapors, soot, fumes, acids, alkalis, toxic chemicals, liquids or gases, waste materials or other irritants, contaminants or pollutants into or upon land, the atmosphere or any water course or body of water; but this exclusion does not apply if such discharge, dispersal, release or escape is sudden and accidental;

In addition to the exclusions listed above which are commonly found in contractual liability forms, any analysis of insurance coverage should determine whether the following exclusions are indicated:

(1) To liability of the indemnitee resulting from his sole negligence;

138

(2) To **bodily injury** or **property damage** included within the **completed operations hazard** or the **products hazard**;

(3) To **property damage** included within

    (a) the **explosion hazard**,

    (b) the **collapse hazard**, or

    (c) the **underground property damage hazard**.

DEFINITIONS OF EXCLUSIONS TERMINOLOGY

In the consideration of the exclusions contained in the contractual liability coverage part, the definitions of certain of the terminology must be recognized. These definitions are included in the contract as a means of further defining the coverage.

1. **Named Insured's Products**

   "**Named insured's products**" means goods or products manufactured, sold, handled or distributed by the **named insured** or by others trading under his name, including any container thereof (other than a vehicle), but "**named insured's products**" shall not include a vending machine or any property other than such container, rented to or located for use of others but not sold.

2. **Explosion Hazard**

   "**Explosion hazard**" includes **property damage** arising out of blasting or explosion. The **explosion hazard** does not include **property damage** (1) arising out of the explosion of air or steam vessels, piping under pressure, prime movers, machinery or power transmitting equipment, or (2) arising out of operations performed for the **named insured** by independent contractors, or (3) included within the **completed operations hazard** or the **underground property damage hazard**, or (4)

139

for which liability is assumed by the **insured** under an **incidental contract.**

3. **Collapse Hazard**

The **"collapse hazard"** includes "structural property damage" as defined herein and **property damage** to any other property at any time resulting therefrom. "Structural property damage" means the collapse of or structural injury to any building or structure due to (1) grading of land, excavating, boring, filling, back-filling, tunnelling, pile driving, cofferdam work or caisson work or (2) moving, shoring, underpinning, raising or demolition of any building or structure or removal or rebuilding of any structural support thereof. The **collapse hazard** does not include **property damage** (1) arising out of operations performed for the **named insured** by independent contractors or (2) included within the **completed operations hazard** or the **underground property damage hazard**, or (3) for which liability is assumed by the **insured** under an **incidental contract.**

4. **Underground Property**

"Underground property damage hazard" includes underground property damage as defined herein and **property damage** to any other property at any time resulting therefrom. "Underground property damage" means **property damage** to wires, conduits, pipes, mains, sewers, tanks, tunnels, any similar property, and apparatus in connection therewith, beneath the surface of the ground or water, caused by and occurring during the use of mechanical equipment for the purpose of grading land, paving, excavating, drilling, boring, filling, back-filling or pile driving. The **underground property damage hazard** does not include **property damage** (a) arising out of operations performed for the **named insured** by independent contractors, or (b) included within the **completed operations hazard,** or (c) for which liability is assumed by the **insured** under an **incidental contract.**

140

5. **Policy Territory**

   "Policy territory" means:

   (a) the United States of America, its territories or possessions, or Canada, or

   (b) international waters or air space, provided the **bodily injury** or **property damage** does not occur in the course of travel or transportation to or from any other country, state or nation, or

   (c) anywhere in the world with respect to damages because of **bodily injury** or **property damage** arising out of a product which was sold for use or consumption within the territory described in paragraph (a) above, provided the original suit for such damages is brought within such territory.

6. **Completed Operations Hazard**

   "Completed operations hazard" includes **bodily injury** and **property damage** arising out of operations or a reliance upon a representation or warranty made at any time with respect thereto, but only if the **bodily injury** or **property damage** occurs after such operations have been completed or abandoned and occurs away from premises owned by or rented to the **named insured**.

   "Operations" include materials, parts or equipment furnished in connection therewith. Operations shall be deemed completed at the earliest of the following times:

   (a) when all operations to be performed by or on behalf of the **named insured** under the contract have been completed, or

   (b) when all operations to be performed by or on behalf of the **named insured** at the site of the operations have been completed, or

   (c) when the portion of the work out of which the injury or damage arises has been put to its intended use by any person or organization other than another contractor or subcontractor engaged in performing operations for a principal as a part of the same project.

Operations which may require further service or maintenance work, or correction, repair or replacement because of any defect or deficiency, but which are otherwise complete, shall be deemed completed.

The **completed operations hazard** does not include **bodily injury** or **property damage** arising out of

(a) operations in connection with the transporation of property, unless the **bodily injury** or **property damage** arises out of a condition in or on a vehicle created by the loading or unloading thereof,

(b) the existence of tools, uninstalled equipment or abandoned or unused materials, or

(c) operations for which the classification stated in the policy or in the company's manual specifies "including completed operations."

Again it must be emphasized that the basic liability contract acts as a vehicle document to carry the contractual coverage. Any evaluation of either without direct consideration of the other can only result in falacious conclusions.

PROVISION OF COVERAGE FOR INTERESTS IN ADDITION TO "INSURED"

In many contracts, an indemnitor is obligated to provide insurance for interests other than for himself. The interests listed below may routinely be added to the indemnitors insurance without charge.

142

1. **Co-owners** but only with respect to their liability as such.

2. **Elective or appointive executive officers or members** of boards or commissions of public and municipal corporations or agencies thereof, on policies covering such corporations or agencies. This rule does not apply to agents or employes of public corporations or agencies whether or not their duties are of an administrative or supervisory nature.

3. **Executors, administrators, trustees or beneficiaries**, or policies covering estates of deceased persons or living trusts.

4. **Fiduciaries.** On policies covering fiduciaries:

   (a) any partner, executive officer, director or stockholder of the named insured while acting within the scope of his duties as such.

   (b) any person or organization while acting as real estate manager for the named insured.

   (c) any co-fiduciary or co-representative of the named insured with respect to his acts or omissions as such.

   (d) with respect to acts or omissions of the named insured in a fiduciary or representative capacity, any person or organization legally responsible therefor.

   (e) any beneficiary, devisee, legatee, ward, heir or distributee of the trust, guardianship or estate, and any co-owner or life tenant of the property, with respect to his acts or omissions as such.

   Coverage for any additional interest under (a), (b), (c), (d), and (e) shall not apply to any executive officer or other-employe with respect to bodily injury to another executive officer or employe of the same employer injured in the course of such employment.

5. **Financial Control.** An individual, group of persons, partnership or corporation which owns or financially controls one or more partnerships or corporations, on policies covering such risks, or corporations or partnerships which are owned or

financially controlled by a single individual, group of persons, partnership or other corporation, on policies covering such controlling interests or interests which they control.

6. **Members of Clubs or unincorporated associations,** on policies covering the club or association but only as respects their liability for activities of the club or association as such, or for activities which are performed on behalf of the club or association other than practice or participation in any game or sport.

7. **Mortgagees, assignees or receivers,** but only for liability as such, on policies covering owners or general lessees.

8. **Oil or Gas Operations—Working Interests.** Co-owners, joint venturers or mining partners having a nonoperating working interest with the insured in oil or gas leases, or policies covering the operators of such leases.

9. **Trustees or members of boards of governors,** or policies covering charitable or educational institutions.

10. **Trustees, members of boards of governors or clergymen,** on policies covering religious institutions.

11. **Husband and wife.**

Additional Charge. All interests other than those enumerated under subdivision (1) through (11) of this rule shall be submitted for rating.

LIMITS OF LIABILITY

When contractual liability insurance is written separately, a separate set of limits applies. These apply independently of the other coverage parts which may be in the same liability policy jacket. This is not true, however, of the incidental contracts as previously discussed because they are a part of the basic coverage. The incidental contract limits are in combination with basic coverages and not separate.

The aggregate limit of liability under Contractual Liability Property Damage Liability applies separately with respect to each project away from premises owned by or rented to the named insured.

Under both bodily injury and property damage liability the language makes it clear that the application of the policy to two or more insureds, claimants or suits does not increase the limits. The intent is to make multiple injury and damage from common or similar conditions subject to the same limit of liability. The policy wording is as follows:

Regardless of the number of (1) **insureds** under this policy, (2) persons or organizations who sustain **bodily injury** or **property damage**, (3) claims made or suits brought on account of **bodily injury** or **property damage**, the Company's liability is limited as follows:

Bodily Injury—The total liability of the company for all damages, including damages for care and loss of services, because of **bodily injury** sustained by one or more persons as the result of any one **occurrence** shall not exceed the limit of **bodily injury** liability stated in the declarations as applicable to "each occurrence."

Property Damage—The total liability of the company for all damages because of all **property damage** sustained by one or more persons or organizations as the result of any one **occurrence** shall not exceed the limit of **property damage** liability stated in the declarations as applicable to "each **occurrence**."

Subject to the above provision respecting "each **occurrence**," the total liability of the company for all damages because of all **property damage** to which this coverage applies shall not exceed the limit of **property damage** liability stated in the declarations as "aggregate." Such aggregate limit of liability applies separately with respect to each project away from premises owned by or rented to the **named insured.**

ADDITIONAL DEFINITIONS

The definition of "contractual liability" included under "Definitions" attempts to make it clear that a warranty of fitness and quality of a product of the named insured or of the workmanlike manner of work completed by or on behalf of the named insured is not part of contractual liability coverage. Products and completed operations liability coverage is needed for this exposure. Warranties excluded under the contractual definitions apply to the named insured's products or works. If the insured assumes the liability of someone else under a designated contract for bodily injury or property damage arising out of that party's products or works, there is coverage.

The additional definition of "suit" already covered is to include "an arbitration proceeding to which the insured is required to submit or to which the insured has submitted with the company's consent." An additional condition now included in the contractual coverage part permits the insurer "to exercise all of the insured's rights in the choice of arbitrators and in the conduct of any arbitration proceeding."

BASIS OF PREMIUM

Premium. All premiums for this policy shall be computed in accordance with the company's rules, rates, rating plans, premiums and minimum premiums applicable to the insurance afforded herein.

Premium designated in this policy as "advance premium" is a deposit premium only which shall be credited to the amount of the earned premium due at the end of the policy period. At the close

146

of each period (or part thereof terminating with the end of the policy period) designated in the declarations as the audit period the earned premium shall be computed for such period and, upon notice thereof to the **named insured**, shall become due and payable. If the total earned premium for the policy period is less than the premium previously paid, the company shall return to the **named insured** the unearned portion paid by the **named insured**.

The **named insured** shall maintain records of such information as is necessary for premium computation, and shall send copies of such records to the company at the end of the policy period and at such times during the policy period as the company may direct.

When used as a premium basis: "cost" means the total cost to any indemnitee with respect to any contract which is insured of all work let or sub-let in connection with each specific project, including the cost of all labor, materials and equipment furnished, used or delivered for use in the execution of such work, whether furnished by the owner, contractor or the subcontractor, including all fees, allowances, bonuses or commissions made, paid or due.

PREMIUM DETERMINATION

The contractual manual contains many varied specific classifications plus many "catch all" classifications. These range from American Institute of Architects—Code 89110 to Utility Agreements indemnification with respect to use of gas, light or power—Code 93164. The varied types of hold harmless agreements make these classifications necessary.

Broad Form

This form indemnifies the other party even where he is solely responsible for the loss and without regard to negligence. You are assuming this liability even when the injury or damage is in no way caused by or contributed to by you, your employes, subcontractors or agents.

This classification applies to agreements requiring complete indemnification of the owner (indemnitee) for all occurrences arising out of the indemnitor's operations without reference to negligence.

Where employes of the indemnitee, other than employes supervising the work, are not engaged in any operations conducted simultaneously at the premises where the construction work is being performed, and, in addition, the circumstances are such as to preclude occurrences resulting from negligence of the indemnitee, except in connection with general supervision by the indemnitee of work performed by the indemnitor, broad form contracts shall be classified and rated as limited form contracts.

Manual Classification

Construction Risk-Broad Form Contracts . . . . . . Code 16281

Limited Form

The limited form holds someone harmless against claims due to your operations, your negligence, or that of your subcontractors.

This classification applies to agreements requiring indemnification of the owner (indemnitee) for occurrences arising out of the indemnitor's operations—no assumption of liability for negligence of the indemnitee except in connection with general supervision of work performed by the indemnitor.

Manual Classification

Construction Agreements —

Construction Risk - Limited form contracts . . . . . . Code 16282

RATING TECHNIQUES

Contractual liability is normally rated on a per $100 of contract cost basis. The words "total cost" mean the total cost to any indemnitee of all work let or sub-let in connection with each specific project, including the cost of all labor, materials and equipment furnished, used or delivered for use in the execution of such work, whether furnished by the owner, contractor or the subcontractor, including all fees, allowances, bonuses or commissions made, paid or due. Separate rates apply for the first $500,000 and all over $1,000,000 of total cost of each specific project.

Basic manual rates are shown for $25,000 per occurrence bodily injury liability and $5,000 per occurrence property damage liability. These are increased by appropriate increased limits factors for the desired limits.

Bodily injury increased limits factors range from 100% of the $25,000 per occurrence rate to 221% for $300,000 per occurrence limit. Table A is the highest rated table because it applies to classifications which contain the letter "s," indicating a hazardous exposure.

Bodily injury increased limits Table B ranges from 100% to 184% of the rate for the same limits and naturally for the less hazardous classes.

Property damage increased limits Table IV factors range from 100% of the $5,000 limit rate to 204% for $50,000 limit where there is no aggregate limit.

Table VII, for use when aggregate limits apply, ranges from 100% to 169% for $50/100,000 property damage limits.

Rating examples for Broad Form, Limited Form and the American Institute of Architects contracts are illustrated below. The premiums represent contracts under which the "total cost" to the indemnitee for all work let or sublet, including the cost of all labor, materials and equipment furnished, used or delivered for use in execution of such work, whether furnished by the owner, contractor or subcontractor, including all fees, allowances, bonuses or commissions made, paid or due.

BROAD FORM Code 16281
($500,000 Contract Cost)

Bodily Injury
.018 rate for $25,000 limit
x1.84 ($300,000 increased limit factor)
.0331 / $300,000 rate
x $500,000 contract cost
$166. Premium

Property Damage
.009 rate for $5,000 limit
x 2.04 ($50,000 increased limit factor)
.0184 / $50,000 rate
x $500,000 contract cost
$92. Premium

LIMITED FORM — Code 16282
($500,000 Contract Cost)

Bodily Injury
.017 rate for $25,000 limit
x 1.84 ($300,000 increased limit factor)
.0313 / $300,000 rate
x $500,000 contract cost
$157. Premium

Property Damage
.008 rate for $5,000 limit
x 2.04 ($50,000 increased limit factor)
.0163 / $50,000 rate
x $500,000 contract cost
$82. Premium

AMERICAN INSTITUTE OF ARCHITECTS—Code 89110
($500,000 Contract Cost)

Bodily Injury
.046 rate for $25,000 limit
x 1.84 ($300,000 increased limit factor)
.0846 / $300,000 rate
x $500,000 contract cost
$423. Premium

Property Damage
.022 rate for $5,000 limit
x 2.04 ($50,000 increased limit factor)
.0449 / $50,000 rate
x $500,000 contract cost
$225. Premium

It should be noted that the rates illustrated are considered only advisory. There is a wide range of rates currently being utilized by various underwriters and their respective cooperative rating organizations.

The majority of insurance carriers utilize the form previously described in detail. These insurance forms are usually categorized as standard contractual liability coverage parts.

Contrarily there are many variations of these standard forms available. The entire text of a non-standard form follows as an illustration of one of the deviations from the standard form.

BLANKET CONTRACTUAL COVERAGE

Webster defines the word blanket: "(1) to cover, or make to apply to, uniformly, despite wide separation or diversity among the elements included, (2) including or covering a group or class; effective or applicable in all instances or contingencies." How does this word blanket work when used in contractual liability insurance? So far, in spite of what some people think, true blanket contractual coverage would be considered very scarce. Some companies exclude Broad Form contracts (sole negligence), some enumerate other types of contracts not covered, others will not write the coverage on certain types of risk and still others just plainly will not write it at all. When blanket coverage is written many companies put a 30 day reporting clause in the policy requiring that hold harmless agreements be reported within 30 days in order to have automatic coverage. Very quickly one can decide that much has to be done to get the blanket in blanket contractual in the proper perspective.

The Insurance Services Office advisory contractual liability insurance blanket form covers written contracts of the type designated in the schedule of the insurance.

In addition, some insurers specifically exclude such contracts as (1) incidental contracts (2) contracts with labor unions and (3) contracts with railroads. Of course incidental contracts are covered in basic liability policies and are excluded here to avoid duplicate coverage. There are objections to labor union contracts on a blanket basis and railroads have catastrophe potential. Underwriters wish to study these before commitment.

When providing blanket coverage, companies usually wish to look at the insured's usual contractual assumptions in advance to determine what types of contract he signs. The rate is also dependent on this. Purchasers of blanket contractual coverage must be made aware of the various limitations and not be lulled into relying on the automatic coverage to take care of them. Agents, brokers and insureds must be alert to find the insurance market which can write the broadest forms and fill their needs.

The ultimate would be to have contractual insurance covering on a blanket basis any contract which a businessman may sign regardless of the degree of liability assumed, from the limited to the very broad. This is not now available, so automatic coverage of contractual assumptions may be viewed as a sort of *semi-blanket* situation instead of blanket.

NON–STANDARD BROAD FORM LIABILITY POLICY
Insuring Agreements and Exclusions

Coverage B. Bodily Injury Liability—Except Automobile.

To pay on behalf of the assured all sums which the assured shall become legally obligated to pay as damages because of bodily injury, sickness or disease, including death at any time resulting therefrom, sustained by any person, irrespective of whether such damages are imposed by law or assumed under contract.

Coverage D. Property Damage Liability—Except Automobile.

153

To pay on behalf of the assured all sums which the assured shall become legally obligated to pay as damages because of injury to or destruction of property (including the loss of use thereof following injury or destruction) irrespective of whether such damages are imposed by law or assumed under contract.

This certificate does not apply:

(A) Under Coverages A and B, expect with respect to liability assumed under contract covered by this certificate, to bodily injury to or sickness, disease or death of any employe of the assured while engaged in the employment of the assured, other than a domestic employe whose injury arises out of an automobile covered by this certificate and for whose injury benefits are not payable or required to be provided under any workmen's compensation law; or to any obligation for which the assured or any company as his insurer may be held liable under any workmen's compensation law;

(B) Under Coverages B and D, except with respect to operations performed by independent contractors, to the ownership, maintenance or use of (1) any aircraft (other than miniature or model aircraft) while in flight, landing, taking off, taxiing or moving under its own power in any manner, or (2) any automobile while away from premises owned, rented or controlled by the named assured;

(C) Under Coverages B and D, to the ownership, maintenance or use, of any vessel owned by the named assured or chartered by the named assured under "bare boat" charter, while such vessel is away from premises owned, rented or controlled by the named assured;

(D) Under Coverages C and D, to any liability of the assured, as an insurer, specifically assumed under contract by the assured for injury to or destruction of property leased or rented to or in the care, custody of control of the assured; but this exclusion shall not apply if the assured would have been liable for such injury, loss or destruction, irrespective of his having assumed the liability of an insurer.

154

(E) Under Coverages C and D, to injury to or destruction of (1) any property while on premises owned, rented or controlled by the assured and held by the assured under any bailment the principal purpose of which is the storage, repair or sale of such property, or (2) any property while being transported in or upon any automobile owned by the assured;

(F) Under Coverage D, to injury to or destruction of (1) goods or products manufactured, sold, handled or distributed or premises alienated by the named assured, if such injury thereto or loss or destruction thereof arises out of the handling or use of or the existence of any condition in such goods, products or premises, or (2) work completed by or for the named assured, if such injury thereto or loss or destruction thereof arises out of faulty or defective workmanship or improper performance of such work;

(G) Under Coverages C and D, damage or destruction caused intentionally by or at the direction of the assured.

Under the insuring agreements such a policy not only provides coverage for damages imposed by law but also for damages assumed under contract. There are no reporting provisions for contracts, so it is automatic. The policy is blanket except for application of its seven main exclusions to contractual liability.

The broad form liability contract, besides providing broader contractual coverage as described above, also furnishes substantially more coverage than the standard comprehensive general liability contract. It has been offered on the London market for a number of years and is marketed by a few domestic carriers. Of course, the risk is very carefully underwritten. The policy carries a small deductible per occurrence and the cost can vary upward from approximate domestic premiums depending upon the nature, loss record, etc., of the risk.

155

OWNER'S OR CONTRACTOR'S PROTECTIVE INSURANCE

Owner's or contractor's protective liability insurance, commonly called independent contractor coverage, has a very important relationship to contractual liability insurance. It covers liability imposed on owners or general contractors for acts arising out of operations of independent contractors or subcontractors or out of the owner's or general contractor's supervisory activities.

An employer of an independent contractor is liable vicariously for the negligence of the contractor under certain circumstances either because of some duty imposed by statute or something that might arise under common law. He can also be liable directly because of negligence such as failure to: (1) inspect the work; (2) employ competent contractors; (3) give reasonable orders; or (4) take precautions to assure that the work will be done safely.

Other than the comprehensive general liability form, coverage for liability of dependent contractors is excluded under most liability forms. An owner or contractor must purchase owner's or contractor's protective liability insurance if he does not have the comprehensive general liability form. The standard insuring agreement in these protective coverages refers to bodily injury or property damage "arising out of operations performed for the named insured by independent contractors and general supervision thereof by the named insured."

Owner's or contractor's protective liability insurance is not a replacement for contractual liability insurance. If there is a hold harmless agreement inflicted, there has to be contractual liability insurance in order to have protection; however, the insured does get a lower rate on his contractual premium if there is a protective policy in force.

There would be little need for hold harmless agreements if the assuming party could offer to furnish this protective coverage for the indemnitee in lieu of accepting a hold harmless clause. In this manner, the indemnitee would have better protection; the assuming party would not have assumed unlimited liability; and the insurance company would be identified as the party solely responsible for adjusting and paying the claims.

The owner should, when considering eliminating the hold harmless agreement, make certain that: (1) he has adequate insurance to cover his own employes for workers' compensation and general liability; (2) his general contractor and all subcontractors are adequately insured; (3) he has owner's or contractor's protective coverage; and (4) make sure that his primary insurance and protective coverage is for the same limits in the same company. This fourth item is very important because this will avoid disputes concerning whether a claim arises out of supervisory acts or non-supervisory acts not connected with the contract job.

SPECIAL INSURANCE APPLICATIONS

Over the course of the past decade, there have been developments which have been designed to provide unique application of the insurance technique to contractual liability situations. Although some of these efforts have the appearance of being desperate, there is enough evidence of their use that a brief discussion follows:

Use of Certificates of Insurance

In the ever changing insurance marketplace for contractual liability insurance, some practitioners are resorting to the practice of attempting to solve their contractual liability problems by acquiring certificates of insurance from the parties to the contract.

There is widespread documentation that indemnitees are content to have certificates which specifically describe the contract under which liability has been transferred and assume that the description of the contract on the certificate provides them with evidence of complete insurance coverage from the indemnitor. It should be noted that the insurance regulators are demanding that the insurers restrict the coverage certificated by the following wording, "This certificate of insurance neither affirmatively or negatively amends, extends, or alters the coverage afforded by these policies".

It is most significant that this restrictive requirement bears directly on the subject of contractual liability insurance coverage. In essence, it redundantly confines the coverage to that provided in the insurance policy. The indemnitee must have some knowledge of the coverage provided in the insurance contract, if he is to have confidence in the certificate. In the absence of this information, the certificate may serve only as a source of misunderstanding and confusion.

The continuing trend toward risk assumption has also created new concerns for those parties providing and accepting certificates of insurance. For those entities who either partially or totally retain the risk arising out of the assumption of liability under contract, it is most difficult for them to provide any acceptable evidence of any available indemnification except that afforded by their respective financial statements. Even in the situations where such risk assumption is employed, there has been some concern that such assumption could bring them under the jurisdiction of the state insurance authorities and be subjected to legal action for practicing "insurance" which would be beyond their corporate charter. It is important that legal opinion be sought before entering such agreements that could result in these consequences.

Additional Insured

There have been situations in which the indemnitee has relied upon being named as an additional insured under the indemnitor's insurance policy as a means of covering the indemnitee's liability under contract. As has been described in this chapter, there is an important consideration for both how this additional interest in the policy is declared and the effect such additional interest could have on the coverage provided.

The major distinction in the manner in which an additional interest is declared hinges on whether the interest is shown as merely an "additional insured" or is shown as an "additional named insured". Reference to the commentary on these two definitions in this chapter will clearly indicate that being shown as an "additional named insured" is preferable, if such inclusion is to be used as a basis of coverage to be provided by the other contracting party.

It is also important to recognize that the inclusion of more than one insured has a radical impact on the coverage provided. The inclusion of more than one insured under the insurance coverage dilutes the coverage to the extent that the limit available in the event of a claim is the total limit available for all insured. In effect, a judgment in excess of the limit of liability available would leave both the parties in an untenable position. The resolution of how the limit would or could be allocated would be most difficult.

A further concern would be that of the effect on the umbrella or excess liability coverage of the two involved parties. The excess carrier relies on the primary coverage available to the party and any dilution of limits of coverage by the addition of any interest to the primary coverage would undermine this reliance on the primary coverage. In addition, there is an inherent obligation to notify the excess carrier of the inclusion of another interest in the primary coverage.

Specification of Incidental Contracts

Another area in which response to the concern regarding contractual liability is the use of the contractual coverage part to cover "incidental" contracts. As indicated in this chapter, these defined incidental contracts are included as covered exposures in the basic liability coverage form and subjected to the terms and conditions of only that basic form.

While an explanation of the desirability of the advantages and disadvantages of specifically including an incidental contract by adding the contractual coverage part would require a complete analysis and comparison of the two coverage parts, it is important to recognize that there is a significant difference in the nature of the coverage afforded. These differences must be evaluated on the basis of the risk situation being considered before a judgment can be made and it is not appropriate to assume such declaration is an advantage in all situations.

It becomes more apparent that the understanding of the proper function of insurance as a risk handling technique is essential in the treatment of the contractual liability exposure. Often efforts to alter the insurance technique to accommodate this exposure only create a more severe exposure to loss.

CHAPTER VI

CONTRACTUAL LIABILITY INSURANCE IN THE 11/85 EDITION OF THE COMMERCIAL GENERAL LIABILITY INSURANCE PROGRAM

The commercial general liability program of Insurance Services Office is comprised of two basic contracts. One retains the familiar "occurrence" trigger (edition date, November, 1985) and the other utilizes a "claims-made" trigger (edition date, February, 1986).[1] We will first discuss the contractual liability insurance provisions as both contracts deal with them, and then we will devote some time to how the "claims-made" contract provisions differ from the "occurrence."

Contractual liability under the 11/85 CGL is treated in the same manner as the 1/73 CGL - that is, it is excluded, though exceptions to the exclusion exist. The new exlcusion language is as follows:

This insurance does not apply to:

b. "Bodily injury" or "property damage" for which the insured is obligated to pay damages by reason of the assumption of liability in a contract or agreement. This exclusion does not apply to liability for damages:

(1) Assumed in a contract or agreement that is an "insured contract;" or

(2) That the insured would have in the absence of the contract or agreement.

1. For convenience hereinafter, the policies comprising the commercial general liability program are referred to as the 11/85 CGL. References to the January, 1973 comprehensive general liability policy are denoted with 1/73 CGL.

161

Note that the language is simplified and we still have two exceptions. We will look at the second exception first since little change has taken place. The previous "warranties" exception has been replaced with this new language. The new exception will provide for the situations dealt with in the previous "warranties" exception, but since it is not limiting the exception to specific *types* of "warranties," it may provide broader coverage.

In the 1/73 edition's first exception, "incidental contracts" were covered automatically. The 11/85 edition provides coverage for "insured contracts" and they are defined in the policy as follows:

    6.   "Insured contract" means:

        a.   A lease of premises;

        b.   A sidetrack agreement;

        c.   An easement or license agreement in connection with vehicle or pedestrian private railroad crossings at grade;

        d.   Any other easement agreement, except in connection with construction or demolition operations on or within 50 feet of a railroad.

        e.   An indemnification of a municipality as required by ordinance, except in connection with work for a municipality;

        f.   An elevator maintenance agreement; or

        g.   That part of any other contract or agreement pertaining to your business under which you assume the tort liability of another to pay damages because of "bodily injury" or "property damage" to a third person or organization, if the contract or agreement is made prior to the "bodily injury" or "property damage" Tort liability means a liability that would be imposed by law in the absence of any contract or agreement.

An "insured contract" does not include that part of any contract or agreement:

a. That indemnifies an architect, engineer or surveyor for injury or damage arising out of:

(1) Preparing, approving or failing to prepare or approve maps, drawings, opinions, reports, surveys, change orders, designs or specifications; or

(2) Giving directions or instructions, or failing to give them, if that is the primary cause of the injury or damage; or

b. Under which the insured, if an architect, engineer or surveyor, assumes liability for injury or damage arising out of the insured's rendering or failing to render professional services, including those listed in a. above and supervisory, inspection or engineering services; or

c. That indemnifies any person or organization for damage by fire to premises rented or loaned to you.

As you can see, the term includes the traditional "incidental contracts" as well as the broadened coverage and additional exclusions from the broad form CGL endorsement, GL 04 04 *and* the GL 99 19 endorsement amending the broad form CGL endorsement. They have now been meshed into one provision in the basic contract and the language has been simplified where possible. Since Chapter V gave definitions of the "incidental contracts," we will only deal with the changes in the new forms. There are some very important changes that have taken place in this definition of "insured contracts" which we will outline along with some points to remember:

163

1. The "third party beneficiary" exclusion, found in the broad form CGL endorsement to the 1/73 CGL, has been deleted. This exclusion was originally introduced to prevent contractually obligated payment of damages to a third party who was not directly involved in the project for a public authority, such as members of the public. The effect of the limitation continues, however, in the second half of paragraph e. of the definition of "insured contract," dealing with "work for a municipality."

2. Note that fire damage legal liability has been excluded under contractual liability coverage since it is covered automatically elsewhere in the basic contract with a separate limit of liability.

3. The most important change is contained in paragraph g. of the definition of "insured contract." This is the paragraph which provides the automatic coverage for assumptions of liability under *any* contract or agreement. The change involves the restriction of coverage to only those assumptions of "tort liability." As paragraph g. explains, "Tort liability means a liability that would be imposed by law in the absence of any contract or agreement." There are many contracts which contain transfer of *non*-tortious liability (mainly those indicating a hold harmless agreement for *all* liability), so it would behoove producers, brokers, and insurers to make it clear to insureds that these will not be covered. For instance, let's assume a subcontractor (an electrician) had to sign a hold harmless agreement with the general contactor, holding the general harmless for all liability arising out of his work on the project. While the electrician was working on and had sole occupancy of the job site, lightning from an electrical storm caused a

164

fire (or perhaps a terrorist exploded a bomb) that destroyed the unfinished building. While the general could, possibly, take some action against the sub due to the language in the hold harmless agreement, the sub's 11/85 CGL policy will not cover this *non-tortious* liability.

In addition, it appears there will be no standard endorsement available which will provide a buy-back of this "non-tortious" liability coverage. Of course, individual insurers may develop and file such an endorsement with the State Insurance Departments, if they desire.

4. We also need to take a look at what is *not* in the new definition of "insured contracts." Remember that the broad form CGL endorsement had five additional exclusions to apply to the broadened contractual liability coverage, but note that under (c) of that form, certain coverage A exclusions are deleted from applying to contractual liability coverages. These are:

    (b) to bodily injury or property damage arising out of the ownership, maintenance, operation, use, loading or unloading of

    (1) any automobile or aircraft owned or operated by or rented or loaned to any insured, or

    (2) any other automobile or aircraft operated by any person in the course of his employment by any insured;

    but this exclusion does not apply to the parking of an automobile on premises owned by, rented to or controlled by the named insured or the ways immediately adjoining, if such automobile is not owned by or rented or loaned to any insured;

(c) to bodily injury or property damage arising out of . . .

    (2) the operation or use of any snowmobile or trailer designed for use therewith;

(d) to bodily injury or property damage arising out of and in the course of the transportation of mobile equipment by an automobile owned or operated by or rented or loaned to any insured;

(e) to bodily injury or property damage arising out of the ownership, maintenance, operation, use, loading or unloading of

    (1) any watercraft owned or operated by or rented or loaned to any insured, or

    (2) any other watercraft operated by any person in the course of his employment by any insured;

but this exclusion does not apply to watercraft while ashore on premises owned by, rented to or controlled by the named insured;

Under the 11/85 edition of the CGL, the deletion of these exclusions is continued for contractual liability coverage by adding a sentence to the individual coverage A exclusions. The biggest change here is that the automobile exclusion is *not* deleted from applying to contractual liability. It is intended that the commercial auto coverage forms provide for this exposure. Contractual liability arising out of the ownership, maintenance or use of aircraft or watercraft will continue to be covered.

DEFINITIONS OF POLICY TERMS APPLICABLE TO CONTRACTUAL LIABILITY

Many of the terms and their definitions have changed in the 11/85 CGL policies. Since there will no longer be a contractual liability policy, as such, with the 11/85 program, we will only deal with those terms in the new commercial general liability forms that appear to have an impact on contractual liability coverage.

3. **Bodily Injury**
"Bodily Injury" means bodily injury, sickness or disease sustained by a person, including death resulting from any of these at any time.

6. **Insured Contract**
This definition was reproduced earlier in the chapter, so it will not be repeated. It should be remembered that while the definition is broader than the "incidental contract" definition found in the 1/73 CGL, it is less broad than the 1/73 CGL with the broad form CGL endorsement since the new forms are restricted to covering the contractual obligation of *tort* liability.

9. **Occurrence**
"Occurrence" means an accident, including continuous or repeated expsure to substantially the same general harmful conditions. Note that the "expected or intended" language found in the 1/73 CGL definition has been moved to Exclusion 2.a. in coverage A. This change simply aids in clarifying that expected *or* intended occurrences are excluded.

12. **Property Damage**
"Property Damage"means:
a. Physical injury to tangible property, including all resulting loss of use of that property; or
b. Loss of use of tangible property that is not physically injured.

13. **Suit**
"Suit means a civil proceeding in which damages because of "bodily injury," "property damage," "personal injury," or "advertising injury" to which this insurance applies are alleged. "Suit" includes an arbitration proceeding alleging such damages to which you must submit or submit with our consent.

EXCLUSIONS APPLICABLE TO CONTRACTUAL LIABILITY

Again, there isn't a separate, self-contained contractual liability policy in the new program, so we will deal with the exclusions which appear to have some impact on contractual liability coverage within the basic contract that also apply to the rest of the coverages within the CGL.

Coverage A. Bodily Injury and Property Damage Liability

    2.   **Exclusions.**

This insurance does not apply to:

(b) "Bodily injury" or "property damage" for which the insured is obligated to pay damages by reason of the assumption of liability in a contract or agreement. This exclusion does not apply to liability for damages:

    (1)   Assumed in a contract or agreement that is an "insured contract"; or

    (2)   That the insured would have in the absence of the contract or agreement.

This is the exclusion which defines the extent of contractual liability coverage being provided in the basic contract.

(c) "Bodily injury" or "property damage" for which any insured may be held liable by reason of:

    (1)   Causing or contributing to the intoxication of any person;

    (2)   The furnishing of alcoholic beverages to a person under the legal drinking age or under the influence of alcohol; or

    (3)   Any statute, ordinance or regulation relating to

the sale, gift, distribution or use of alcoholic beverages.

This exclusion applies only if you are in the business of manufacturing, distributing, selling, serving or furnishing alcoholic beverages.

The liquor liability exclusion has been changed to provide broader coverage in a contractual situation. The "or his indemnitee" language from the 1/73 CGL has been removed which means that he 11/85 CGL will provide coverage for the contractual obligation of the insured's indemnitee, *whether or not* the insured or his indemnitee is "in the business of manufacturing, distributing, selling, serving or furnishing alcoholic beverages." Adequacy of the limits of liability continue to be of concern.

(d)   Any obligation of the insured under a workers compensation, disability benefits or unemployment compensation law or any similar law.

No apparent change has taken place in this exclusion. While the 1/73 CGL and contractual liability coverage part appear to have provided coverage for *contractually* obligated payments of someone else's workers compensation obligations, the 11/85 CGL will *not*, unless it can be proved that the assumption of liability was an assumption of someone else's *tort* liability.

(e)   "Bodily injury" to:

(1)   An employee of the insured arising out of and in the course of employment by the insured; or

(2)   The spouse, child, parent, brother or sister of that employee as a consequence of (1) above.

This exclusion applies:

(1)   Whether the insured may be liable as an employer or in any other capacity; and

169

(2) To any obligation to share damages with or repay someone else who must pay damages because of the injury.

This exclusion does not apply to liability assumed by the insured under an "insured contract."

This exclusion is similar to the 1/73 CGL employer's liability exclusion as amended by ISO endorsement GL 00 32 (04 84). The biggest difference is that the 1/73 exclusion indicates that it does not apply to liability assumed by the insured under an *incidental contract*. The 11/85 exclusion provides coverage if the liability is assumed under an *insured contract*, and as we've already discussed, "insured contract" is a slightly broader term than "incidental contract," but it is less broad than the 1/73 CGL with the broad form CGL endorsement attached.

(g) "Bodily injury" or "property damage" arising out of the ownership, maintenance, use of entrustment to others of any aircraft, "auto" or watercraft owned or operated by or rented or loaned to any insured.

Use includes operation and "loading or unloading."

This exclusion does not apply to:

(1) Watercraft while ashore on premises you own or rent;

(2) A watercraft you do not own that is:

(a) Less than 26 feet long; and

(b) Not being used to carry persons or property for a charge;

(3) Parking an "auto" on, or on the ways next to, premises you own or rent, provided the "auto" is not owned by or rented or loaned to you or the insured;

170

(4) Liability assumed under any ''insured contract'' for the ownerhsip, maintenance or use of aircraft or watercraft; or

(5) ''Bodily injury'' or ''property damage'' arising out of the operation of any of the equipment listed in paragraph f.(2) or f.(3) of the definition of ''mobile equipment'' (Section VI.8.).

The exemption of the exclusion for aircraft or water-craft essentially provides the same coverage as the 1/73 CGL with the broad form CGL endorsement. The important aspect of this exclusion is the fact that automobile liability assumed under contract is *excluded* in the 11/85 CGL. The reasoning for this exclusion is that the commercial automobile policy will contain provisions for covering automobile contractual liability. This exclusion simply prevents duplicate coverage.

(i) ''Bodily injury'' or ''property damage'' due to war, whether or not declared, or any act or condition incident to war. War includes civil war, insurrection, rebellion or revolution. This exclusion applies only to liability assumed under a contract or agreement.

War damage continues to be excluded.

(j) ''Property damage'' to:

(1) Property you own, rent, or occupy;

(2) Premises you sell, give away or abandon, if the ''property damage'' arises out of any part of those premises;

(3) Property loaned to you;

(4) Personal property in you care, custody or control;

171

(5) That particular part of real property on which you or any contractors or subcontractors working directly or indirectly on your behalf are performing operations, if the "property damage" arises out of those operations; or

(6) That particular part of any property that must be restored, repaired or replaced because "your work" was incorrectly performed on it.

Paragraph (2) of this exclusion does not apply if the premises are "your work" and were never occupied, rented or held for rental by you.

Paragraphs (3), (4), (5) and (6) of this exclusion do not apply to liability assumed under a sidetrack agreement.

Paragraph (6) of this exclusion does not apply to "property damage" included in the "products-completed operations hazard."

This exclusion has been simplified and reworded, but very little has changed with regard to contractual liability. It is, in essence, the same coverage as the 1/73 CGL with the broad form CGL endorsement attached. Minor changes have been made, however. Damage to personal property on elevators is now excluded, treating this property like all other personal property in the care, custody or control of the insured. Also, a broadening of coverage was made to allow coverage for damage to *real* property in the insured's care, custody or control.

Coverage B. Personal and Advertising Injury Liability.

    2.   **Exclusions.**

This insurance does not apply to:

    (a)   "Personal injury" or "advertising injury:"

172

(1) Arising out of oral or written publication of material, if done by or at the direction of the insured with the knowledge of its falsity;

(2) Arising out of oral or written publication of material whose first publication took place before the beginning of the policy period;

(3) Arising out of the willful violation of a penal statute or ordinance committed by or with the consent of the insured; or

(4) For which the insured has assumed liability in a contract or agreement. This exclusion does not apply to liability for damages that the insured would have in the absence of the contract or agreement.

This reworded and simplified exclusion continues to exclude contractually obligated personal injury or advertising injury liability losses. In addition, language has been added which clarifies that coverage will not be voided if the insured assumes liability under a contract, and the insured would have that liability without the existence of the contract.

(b) "Advertising injury" arising out of:

(1) Breach of contract, other than misappropriation of advertising ideas under an implied contract:

This exclusion appears only to be put in simplified language.

Coverage C. Medical Payments.

2. **Exclusions.**

We will not pay expenses for "bodily injury:"

(g) Excluded under Coverage A.

This exclusion appears only to be a simplification of the existing exclusion in the broad form CGL endorsement.

As was stated in Chapter V, contractual liability is an integral part of the CGL coverage part, and even more so with the 11/85 CGL since contractual liability is built into the basic contract. As such, all policy conditions, definitions, and exclusions play a part in defining the actual coverage in a specific contractual liability loss. While we have outlined and discussed some important contractually related exclusions in the 11/85 CGL, there are additional exclusions which could possibly effect a limitation of coverage in a particular situation. It is recommended that all of these exclusions be reviewed in light of each insured's or prospective insured's unique situation.

LIMITS OF LIABILITY

The 11/85 CGL policies contain annual aggregate limits over either the occurrence or claims-made limits for *all* coverages in the contracts. There is a general aggregate to apply to all coverages other than products/completed operations. A separate aggregate will apply to products/completed operations losses. The 1/73 CGL basic contracts only use aggregates over BI occurrence limits for products/completed operations exposures and over PD occurrence limits for M&C and products/completed operations exposures. The 1/73 contractual liability coverage part uses an aggregate only for contractual property damage exposures. The 1/73 broad form CGL endorsement uses the limits of liability of the basic contract, with three additional separate limits: a per occurrence limit for fire damage legal liability; an each person limit for premises medical payments; and an aggregate limit (over the bodily injury occurrence limit in the basic contract) for personal injury and advertising injury liability.

174

The biggest impact of this new aggregate is on M&C BI exposures and OL&T BI and PD exposures. Since contractual coverage is built into the basic contracts, the coverage A occurrence (or claims-made) limits with their limiting aggregates will apply to contractual as well as other premises/operations exposures. Adequacy of policy limits will become more of a concern now that these aggregates apply to all policy coverages. A manual rule provision allows the insurer to reinstate the impaired aggregate limit, if requested, and at an additional premium to be determined by the insurer. As claims start mounting on a particular insured, it would behoove the agent or broker to keep tabs on the dwindling aggregate and make sure the insured understands that available coverage is being reduced each time a claim is paid. A quotation for reinstatement of the limits should be pursued and a written offer made to the insured. This offer will help protect the insured as well as the agent/broker.

OTHER CHANGES

It needs to be emphasized that ISO is not providing a contractual liability coverage part or endorsement to replace the current "designated contracts only" form. The reliance will be on the basic blanket contractual liability coverage found in the policy. Should an insurer need the capability of picking the contracts it wants to insure (to the exclusion of others) for a particular insured, it will need to develop its own schedule endorsement, and file it with the appropriate state regulatory authorities.

The only contractual liability endorsement available in the 11/85 CGL program is one which removes coverage for any contractually assumed tort liability and leaves only the traditional "incidental contracts" covered. Also note that coverage under this amendment is limited to *written* "insured contracts."

The collapse, explosion, and underground property damage exclusions have been totally eliminated, thereby providing coverage under the basic policy as well as covering any contractual obligation assumed under an "insured contract." These property damage exclusions *may* be added by endorsement for specific applications.

Contracts or agreements covered under "insured contracts" may be written *or* verbal, unless the above mentioned limiting endorsement is attached.

Leases or easements of waterfront property continue to be covered under the 11/85 CGL provisions, as well as liability assumed under any "insured contract" for the ownership, maintenance or use of watercraft.

SPECIAL "CLAIMS-MADE" CONSIDERATIONS

As mentioned earlier, the 11/85 CGL will have two versions: one which will use the traditional "occurrence" coverage trigger and a second which is identical except it will utilize a "claims-made" coverage trigger. There are some considerations to keep in mind when issuing a "claims-made" contract to an insured when there is contractual liability exposure.

The 11/85 claims-made CGL defines the coverage trigger as follows:

> "This insurance applies to "bodily injury" and "property damage" only if a claim for damages because of the "bodily injury" or "property damage" is first made against any insured during the policy period."

At this point, it makes no difference when the bodily injury or property damage *occurred*, as long as the claim is made during the policy period. Therefore, if a contractual liability claim is made during the claims-made policy period for bodily injury which actually occurred in 1925, and the contract fits the definition of "insured contract," then the policy will respond. There can be some limitations to this coverage which will be discussed later.

In addition, there is a revised "other insurance" condition which indicates that this coverage applies on a primary basis, but will also respond as excess coverage if there is other insurance that could apply. If an "occurrence" contractual liability policy had been written in 1925 that applied to the above loss example, it would pay the loss until its limits were depleted, and then the claims-made policy would come in and respond with its limits, if needed.

Claims must simply be "received and recorded" in some manner. This means the injured party can make a claim verbally, as long as the agent or insurer "receives and records" the claim.

EXTENDED REPORTING PERIODS

When a claims-made policy expires, no further coverage is available from that policy, since claims can no longer be *made* during the policy period. When a claims-made policy expires and a renewal is issued or a new claims-made policy is issued by another insurer, the expired policy provides no coverage at all, but the new contract picks up the exposure. Under a situation where claims-made policies annually replace expiring claims-made policies with *no limitations* to the broad coverage being provided, there appear to be no gaps in coverage. However, as we will see later, there are limiting provisions insurers may use which could cause a gap in coverage. In nearly all of these situations, when the gap manifests itself, there is an additional policy provision which will help to protect the insured. It is a separate section of the claims-made policy entitled "Section V - Extended Reporting Periods." The extended reporting period provision provides the following extension of coverage:

4. Extended Reporting Periods do not extend the policy period or change the scope of coverage provided. They apply only to claims for "bodily injury" or "property damage" that occur before the end of the policy period (but not before the Retroactive Date, if any, shown in the Declarations).

   Claims for such injury or damage which are first received and recorded during the Basic Extended Reporting Period (or during the Supplemental Extended Reporting Period, if it is in effect) will be deemed to have been made on the last day of the policy period.

   Once in effect, Extended Reporting Periods may not be cancelled.

There are three extended reporting periods provided. The first two are considered the *basic* extended reporting periods and are defined as follows:

2. A Basic Extended Reporting Period is automatically provided without additional charge. This period starts with the end of the policy period and lasts for:

   a. Five years for claims arising out of an "occurrence" reported to us, not later than 60 days after the end of the policy period, in accordance with paragraph 2.a. of SECTION IV - COMMERCIAL GENERAL LIABILITY CONDITIONS; or

   b. Sixty days for all other claims.

      The Basic Extended Reporting Period does not apply to claims that are covered under any subsequent insurance you purchase, or that would be covered but for exhaustion of the amount of insurance applicable to such claims.

The first basic extended reporting period must be "triggered" in two ways. There must be occurrences, or incidents, *during* the policy period which *may* result in a claim at a later date—the details of which the insured has promptly relayed to the insurer, but no later than 60 days after the policy expiration date. The second necessary "trigger" of this extension is that there must be no subsequent coverage that could apply to this claim. Note also that this basic extended reporting period will not apply even in a situation where you had a notified occurrence, and the claim was made during a subsequent claims-made policy that would pay the claim except for the fact that the limit of liability has been exhuasted. Again, adequacy of the limits of liability are a major concern.

The second basic extended reporting period simply extends the reporting period for sixty days for all other claims not provided for in the first basic extended reporting period. These claims are the "true" I.B.N.R. losses.

These basic extended reporting periods are automatic, when the specified conditions are met, and are at no additional cost.

The third extended reporting period is called the *supplemental* exended reporting period and is defined as follows:

3. A Supplemental Extended Reporting Period of unlimited duration is available, but only by an endorsement and for an extra charge. This supplemental period starts:

a. Five years after the end of the policy period for claims arising out of an "occurrence" reported to us, not later than 60 days after the end of the policy period, in accordance with paragraph 2.a. of SECTION IV-COMMERCIAL GENERAL LIABILITY CONDITIONS; or

b. Sixty days after the end of the policy period for all other claims.

The supplemental extended reporting period is *not* automatic (however, its availability is guaranteed), it must be purchased (the additional premium is (a) rated, but capped at 200% of the policy premium), and it is effective for an unlimited time period. If an insured goes out of business or is not able to renew a claims-made policy and is forced to switch to an occurrence policy, this unlimited reporting period should definitely be purchased. Note that the request for this option must be made in writing, within 60 days after the expiration date of the policy.

An important aspect of these three extended reporting periods are their treatments of the aggregate limits. The two *basic* extended reporting periods utilize the remainder of the aggregate limits available at the expiration date of the policy. If this limit is impaired, it *can* be reinstated at an additional premium.

The *supplemental* extended reporting period, however, has a built-in reinstatement of the aggregate limits when it is purchased. This reinstated aggregate only begins when the supplemental extended reporting period begins, which is described in the quotation above.

RETROACTIVE DATES

Another provision which can have a dramatic effect on contractual liability coverage is the retroactive date provision. The basic insuring agreement of the claims-made policy makes the following statement:

> "This insurance does not apply to "bodily injury" or "property damage" which occurred before the Retroactive Date, if any, shown in the Declarations or which occurs after the policy period."

The Declarations Page has a blank for a retroactive date to be inserted, if the underwriter so desires. Without a date inserted, the claims-made policy will respond to contractual liability *occurrences* (as well as all GL occurrences) no matter how long ago they occurred, as long as the written claim for damages is *made* during the policy period. The retroactive date provision simply provides a "cap" as to how far back the policy will go to pick up occurrences for claims-made losses. For example, let's assume a claims-made policy was issued for a term of 1/1/85 - 1/1/86, with a retroactive date of 1/1/85. Let's also assume a contractual liability loss *occurred* 10/15/83 and the claim for damages was not made until 2/15/85. Since the loss occurred *prior* to the 1/1/85 retroactive date, no coverage will be provided by the claims-made policy even though the claim was made during the policy period. If there were no retroactive date, or the date selected was prior to the actual occurrence, then coverage would have been provided.

If an insured has been written on a claims-made policy with no retroactive date and then at renewal one is inserted, a gap in coverage will arise. At this point, the insured would automatically have the basic extended reporting periods and should consider purchasing the supplemental extended reporting period endorsement to protect himself for contractual (as well as other GL) exposures during those years coverage was supplied by a claims-made policy prior to the new retroactive date. This recommendation would also

181

apply in the situation where a retroactive date is *advanced* upon renewal or with a new policy.

In addition to this policy retroactive date provision, there is an endorsement available for the underwriter's use which allows the underwriter to exclude coverage for: a specific "accident" which has occurred, but the claim for damages has not actually been made yet; a specific "location"; a specific "product"; or a specific aspect of the insured's "work." It is understandable that an underwriter would not want to issue a claims-made policy knowing in advance that a claim was going to be made during the policy period for an accident that has already occurred; or, perhaps the only way the underwriter will provide GL coverage is if a very hazardous location or product is excluded. It appears, therefore, that this endorsement is necessary for the claims-made policy to enhance availability. From a contractual liability standpoint, "accidents," "products," and the insured's "work" which could be the subject of a contract could easily be involved in such an exclusion, and it is important to keep that in mind.

If this exclusion is used, the extended reporting periods should be utilized to protect the insured. If the exclusion is applied on a renewal by the same insurer, that company must offer a special supplemental extended reporting period endorsement which specifically applies to the "accident," "products," or "work" being excluded. If the exclusion is applied by a new carrier, the previous carrier should offer the full supplemental extended reporting period endorsement.

It cannot be emphasized enough that the 11/85 CGL contracts are completely different from the 1/73 CGL and must be understood fully to prevent problems for the insurer, agent, or insured. As has been said previously about the 1/73

182

CGL contractual liability coverage part, one must study the contractual liability coverage in the 11/85 CGL as being an integral part of the CGL coverage part. All conditions, exclusions and coverage grants play a part in molding contractual coverage for a particular insured.

PREMIUM DETERMINATION

In addition to the complete overhaul in the way contractual liability coverage is written, and the simplification of policy wording, ISO also simplified the premium determination rules. Actually, all rules, rates and classifications for contractual liability have been removed entirely. Like the coverage being built into the basic contract, the contractual liability rate has been built into the premises/operations base rate. There are no contractual classification systems, rating bases, or rates to deal with.

As with the coverage forms, the ISO rules may be accepted, rejected or modified by an individual insurer, so it is important for all parties involved to understand fully how an individual insurer intends to approach contractual liability coverage.

OWNER'S OR CONTRACTOR'S PROTECTIVE INSURANCE

Chapter V discussed the details of, and need for, this coverage. The 11/85 CGL continues this coverage with very little change.

SPECIAL INSURANCE APPLICATIONS

In addition to the discussion of owner's or contractor's protective insurance, Chapter V described techniques used by some practitioners to enhance their protection against assumed liability. The comments on the use of certificates of liability, additional insureds, and specification of incidental contracts continue to be appropriate when dealing with the 11/85 CGL.

CHAPTER VII

CASE STUDY

At this point in an analysis of the form and effect of hold harmless agreements and the typical insurance response to such liability, it is important to actually see a case in which many of these considerations are indicated. The case illustrated is in fact actual in every respect and no changes in facts have been made for any particular emphasis on any section of the book. It is most important that the reader follow the sequence of events carefully and he must imagine himself as one of the parties involved either as owner, general contractor, subcontractor, or attorney for any of these, or as the insurance agent or broker for either of the first three parties indicated.

The contract in question involved the testing of certain mechanical equipment which had been installed by the general contractor for its acceptability for pre-established noise level standards. The owner and general contractor had entered a standard AIA contract with the indemnity provisions unaltered. The general contractor recognized at the outset that his organization could not perform the testing function required, but he also believed that such testing could be performed by a suitable subcontractor who specialized in this type of work.

As the installation progressed, the general contractor began his efforts to locate and to contract with a subcontractor to perform these services. He soon discovered that such contractors were most difficult to locate and that his only good source would be the use of a consulting engineering firm. Once he located a competent firm, he found that they were willing to do the job, but almost as an accommodation to him. The contract price for the testing ran less than $10,000, so the engineering firm demonstrated only casual interest in the job.

At this point, the general contractor had his attorney draw a contract for use with the subcontractor. He attached this contract to his usual purchase order agreement and forwarded it to the subcontractor for signature. The technical aspects of the contract were evaluated by the subcontractor and found to be acceptable.

Although making no claim to have any particular expertise on indemnity provisions, the subcontractor phoned his insurance agent and asked him to look over the contract. It is noteworthy that the contract document itself and not the purchase order to which it was attached was initially shown to the agent. The contract was preprinted and the agent located under paragraph 16, entitled INDEMNITY, INSURANCE, the hold harmless clause which read as follows:

The Subcontractor hereby assumes entire responsibility and liability for any and all damage or injury of any kind or nature whatever (including death resulting therefrom) to all persons, whether employes of the Subcontractor or otherwise, and to all property caused by, resulting from, arising out of or occurring in connection with the execution of the work by the Subcontractor, and if any claims for such damage or injury (including death resulting therefrom) be made or asserted, whether or not such claims are based upon general contractor's, its contractors', if any, or the owner's alleged active or passive negligence or participation in the wrong or upon any alleged breach of any statutory duty or obligation on the part of the general contractor, the Subcontractor agrees to indemnify and save harmless, general contractor, its contractor, if any, the owner, their officers, agents, servants and employes from and against any and all such claims, and further from and against any and all loss, cost, expense, liability, damage or injury, including legal fees and disbursements, that general contractor, its officers, agents, servants and employes may directly or indirectly sustain, suffer or incur as a result thereof and the Subcontractor agrees to and does hereby assume, on behalf of general contractor, their officers, agents, servants and employes, the defense of any action at law or in equity which may be brought against general contractor, its contractor, if any, their officers, agents, servants or employes, arising by reason of such claims and

186

to pay on behalf of general contractor, the owner, their officers, agents, servants and employes, upon demand of either of them, the amount of any judgment that may be entered against them, individually, jointly or severally, their officers, agents, servants or employes in any such action. In the event that any such claims, loss, cost, expense, liability, damage or injury arise or are made, asserted or threatened against general contractor, the owner, their officers, agents, servants or employes, general contractor shall have the right to withhold from any payments due or to become due to the Subcontractor an amount sufficient in its judgment to protect and indemnify it, its contractor, if any, the owner, their officers, agents, servants and employes from and against any and all such claims, loss, cost, expense, liability, damage or injury, including legal fees and disbursements, or general contractor, in its discretion, may require the Subcontractor to furnish a surety bond satisfactory to general contractor guaranteeing such protection, which bond shall be furnished by the Subcontractor within five (5) days after written demand has been made therefor.

When the agent completed a quick review of the provision, he said, "I sure hope you have built yourself a lot of fat in this contract, because this is a toughy."

His client replied, "I think we are in good shape because this work is simple for us and, as a matter of fact, we have one of the best engineers in the country doing this type analysis and testing."

"Of course, only you can make a judgment on the technical aspects of the job and only you can determine how many dollars you need to make a buck, but this agreement you are about to sign may make the dollars look like peanuts," sighed the agent. He continued, "These guys are really laying the wood to you by passing on all their liability to you at the outset and then are coming back with this bit of holding back payment to you almost at their discretion, so you may want to take another look at this whole deal before putting your name on the line."

"Darn it, you guys are always complicating life," replied the subcontractor. He questioned the agent, "Why is it that I have a staff of engineers who all have PhD's, the most advanced equipment available, and want to do a simple little consulting job, and this jingle-jangle insurance becomes an issue?"

A little agitated the agent responded, "Jingle-jangle insurance is not the question here . . . we don't create the problems, we only attempt to point out to you some problems we can identify and to relate the insurance response to identified problems. What you do is your business, so, if it is your choice, just sign the contract and let the chips fall where they may."

A short silence ensued.

At this point, the two men began to laugh. They had a degree of respect for each other and both realized that the problem could not be resolved if communications degenerated any further. The subcontractor broke the silence by saying, "O.K., so I'm sorry I called your profession jingle-jangle. Let's get serious and see what we can come up with that will make sense."

Now that the agent recognized the problem was being thrown at him again, he said, "Let's start over. Let me see the whole document and I'll ask you to make me a copy of certain portions of the contract so I can go back to the office and take a good look."

The contractor agreed and said, "By the way, this document is attached to a purchase order form. Do you want to see it?"

"Of course," replied the agent, "if it's a part of the contract, we need to see it all."

The subcontractor passed the purchase order over his desk to the agent and said, "Here it is. Look it over while I have a copy of the contract made for you."

The agent read the purchase order carefully. On the reverse side and in extremely small print he found the following verbiage:

INDEMNITY. Seller hereby agrees to indemnify Buyer for any loss, expense, recovery or settlement, including counsel fees and costs of defense, which arise from any demand, claim (whether frivlous or not) or suit which may be asserted or brought against Seller or Buyer as a result of any injury or damage to any person or persons (including death) or property (i) allegedly caused by, resulting from, arising out of, or occurring in connection with the furnishing of any goods, equipment or services or the performance or preparation for performance of any of the work or any duties of the Seller hereunder, or incidental or pertaining thereto, and (ii) whether or not such injury or damage is due to or chargeable to any alleged negligence of Buyer, the site owner or any contractor or subcontractor under a contract for which the goods or services herein ordered are required, or the alleged negligence of any employe of Buyer, site owner or aforesaid contractor or subcontractor, including, but not limited to, any claim based on liability without fault for injury caused by defective goods supplied by Seller. Seller also agrees to assume responsibility for and to indemnify Buyer for payment of any expenses, costs (including delay costs), direct and consequential damages, penalties, taxes or assessments (including punitive damages), including counsel fees and costs of defense, which may be imposed or incurred (i) under any Federal, state, or local law, ordinance or regulation upon or with respect to any compensation of any person employed by Seller, and (ii) under any Federal, state, or local law, ordinance or regulation upon or with respect to discrimination in employment against any individual employed by Seller on the basis of race, color, religion, sex, or natural origin.

When the subcontractor returned to his office with a copy of the contract, the agent said, "Those rascals are really after you. They have an additional clause here on the back side of the purchase order agreement which makes the other clause look innocuous by comparison." He continued, "This does the best job on you of any hold harmless clause I've ever seen. Boy, this has it all—punitive damage—Occupational Safety and Health Act—consequential damages—loss of market—and even sex."

"Sex?"

"Yes sir, up to and including sex," chuckled the agent.

"Maybe you insurance types aren't all bad, if you can dig out sex in an indemnity clause," snorted the subcontractor.

The apparent gravity of the whole subject was beginning to impress the subcontractor. He now recognized the tremendous importance of the hold harmless provisions and the effect that their application could have not only on the job in question, but also the consequences they might have on the whole future of his company. All of a sudden he wanted quick, simple answers for the complicated problem and asked, "What are my alternatives? What should I do now?"

"Well, let's look at the possibility of applying a little management technique to the problem and see if we can find a satisfactory solution for you," answered the agent. "Some of the possibilities may sound strange to you, but let's get started." The agent requested, "Why don't you jot down these alternatives and we can consider each on it's own merits."

The brain storming session was on. Both knew that a decision had to be reached without further delay. Both became intense. The agent started, "The most obvious solution is to just not sign the contract because there was no problem before the contract came up. It may not sound reasonable to you, since you have already spent considerable time on getting the work done to get started on the job, but it's not too late to just write him a letter and withdraw entirely."

"That's a thought," replied the subcontractor, "but let's just hold that one for a minute and try something else."

"Well, let's consider the other extreme," counseled the agent. "You could always sign the contract and take your chances by assuming all the risks yourself."

"No way that you can convince me that that is a reasonable approach," retorted the subcontractor. "This little job doesn't mean that much to me."

These decisions to neither avoid entering the contract nor to assume the liabilities created by the contract gave the discussion new meaning. A decision had to be reached which would be fair to both parties to the contract. Logic dictated that they would have to call on an attorney for his advice on the moderation of the language in the contract.

"Has your attorney seen this contract?", the agent asked.

"No, but I'm going to get the whole thing to him this afternoon," answered the subcontractor.

"Good," replied the agent. "Why don't you ask him to do the following for you:

"First, please ask him to check the state statutes to see if there have been changes which may affect the contract language because many states have passed such legislation; then

"Secondly, ask him to evaluate these contract provisions as they relate to your insurance coverage, and

191

"Thirdly, to suggest terminology which would be acceptable for you."

The subcontractor contacted his attorney who shared the insurance agent's concern with indemnity provisions in the contract. In checking, he also found a statute which prohibited certain of the provisions contained in the hold harmless agreement, and he suggested the following clause to replace those in the contract:

Subcontractor hereby agrees that he will at all times hereafter indemnify and save harmless general contractor from all loss or damage which he may sustain by reason of injury to any person due to the negligent or willful act of the Subcontractor or the servants or agents of the Subcontractor in the performance of the said Subcontract, including defending, at its own expense, such claims as may be asserted for loss or damage against general contractor arising out of Subcontractor's performance of the said Subcontract.

In a conversation between the attorney for the general contractor—who had written the original contract—and the subcontractor in which the substitution of contract language was agreed upon, the attorney indicated, "I'm sorry we caused you so much trouble, but most often no one ever questions the contract form which is to our advantage. We are agreeable to having the clauses substituted, but you will agree that, had you not found them, my client would have been in an awfully good position."

CONCLUSION

Fortunately, this case illustrates the handling of an unacceptable indemnity clause BEFORE the contract was signed. With the attitude of the attorney of the indemnitee prevailing, any effort to accomplish these results AFTER the contract had been signed probably would have been futile.

CHAPTER VIII

SUMMARY

The use of hold harmless agreements by parties to a contract seems to be employed in practically every facet of contract activity within the economy. Their use may either be intended to serve a legal purpose for which no other technique satisfies as well or it may simply be the result of one of the parties anxiousness to make a sale. It would appear the circumstances surrounding their employment would actually either justify their use or indicate that their use serves only as another consideration in a contract, the cost of which to the indemnitor may be difficult to determine.

The ability of one of the parties to secure contractual indemnity as a supplementary condition to a contract obviously leads to some misunderstanding of the result of such indemnification. This is true because the value of the indemnification directly relates to the ability of the indemnitor to satisfy the demands of the injured party.

Although the legal climate is permissive, the courts do recognize the fallibility of the unreasonable and promiscuous use of contracts to transfer liability; however, the evidence of the written contract itself affords the courts little latitude when the intent is clear from the language and the purpose of the agreement. Such contracts are usually enforceable athough strictly construed if the transfer does not conflict with any statute or public policy.

The trend which has been established to restrict the use of hold harmless agreements through legislative means seems to be gaining some momentum. The limited success already recorded indicates that this approach has already become a significant source for a statutory reevaluation of the entire treatment of indemnity agreements.

It is easily seen when a variety of agreements are analyzed that the identification of the assumption of liability within a contract is at best demanding. The presentation of a series of agreements also indicates that they are to be found in practically every type of contract. The specimens shown in this study were not chosen to reflect the most desirable or undesirable type agreements, but were chosen to indicate some of the more commonly used agreements by a variety of industries.

The treatment of risk arising out of contractual obligations does not differ from risk situations which may arise from any source. The primary difference is that they are created contractually; therefore, the identification and evaluation of the exposure must be related to all the parties involved in the creation of the contract. In essence, the handling of this exposure must be a joint action with all the departments within the organization which are involved with the performance of the contract, since it is an obligation for the firm in its entirety. It is obvious that proper handling of this risk must be the result of adequate pre-planning and an organized program to identify the exposure and to react to the risk.

While contractual liability insurance is recognized as a primary means of handling the risk of assumed liability, its very nature limits its application to all the exposures which may be legally assumed and which are economically insurable. It should be noted that liability insurance itself is a funding mechanism for liability incurred, but limitations and exclusions are necessary. It is for this reason that it is so important that the coverage provided for this exposure be fully understood by the indemnitor. Too often, this simply is not true. Recent developments indicate that the insurance regulatory authorities are insisting that certificates of insurance not be drawn which will agree to protect, defend and hold a party free and unharmed *whatsoever* resulting in connection with the performance of the described work by the other party. The coverage provided and certified must be restricted to the contents of the liability coverage form providing the coverage. It is apparent that the advice of competent insurance practitioners is tantamount to proper use and understanding of the insurance technique of handling the assumed liability risk through insurance.

It is also apparent that the consequence of the assumption of liability under contract may be so severe that the other advantages created by the contract are overshadowed. In these situations, it would seem reasonable that the parties to the contract expunge this condition from the contract in exchange for renegotiation of other aspects of the contract. It does not seem appropriate that a subject which is so controversial outside the contract become such an essential element within the contract.

It is most important that this study reveal that the assumption of liability under contract is to be treated as a most serious consideration, since it obligates the assets of the indemnitor. It is also most important that proper effort be exerted by contracting parties to become aware of such assumption and the importance of seeking competent risk advice.

A sincere attempt has been made in this study to point out the nature, ramifications, peculiarities and dangers incurred in the contractual field. A pleasing and beneficial result of this research would be the initiation by the parties concerned with hold harmless agreements of a program to be used during the negotiation stage of contracts which would provide understanding and avoidance of the problems pointed out in this book. Associations of architects, contractors, subcontractors, building owners, manufacturers, wholesalers, retailers, transporters, utilities and others could render all industry a service by promoting and supporting such an effort.

Since this study was originally concluded in 1968, there is evidence that the matter treated has been made a focal point for the concerned efforts of many. This evidence indicates that unselfish cooperation among interested groups has placed the contractual assumption of another's liability in a much clearer perspective. If this trend continues, the ignorant will be made aware; the indifferent become concerned and those in dispute, mutually understanding.

INDEX

199